Rhododendrons and Azaleas

ANDREA KÖGEL

Series Editor:
LESLEY YOUNG

MEREHURST

Introduction and Contents

Few of us are impervious to the beauty of rhododendrons or azaleas in full bloom, showing a profusion of flowers and an almost infinite range of colours. Even a solitary shrub will enhance the corner of a garden, balcony or patio, no matter whether it is a vigorous 2-m (6½ ft) shrub or a delicate dwarf variety – the wonderful colours will delight anew every year.

This well-illustrated guide will introduce you to the wide range of these exquisite ornamental shrubs by providing all the information you need to know about the different groups of rhododendrons and azaleas. A "flowering calendar" and plant descriptions illustrated in full colour will help you to choose the right plants for your garden or patio and to discover your own favourite varieties. Clear instructions are given on rhododendron cultivation so that your shrubs will thrive and produce masses of blossom each year. Step-by-step illustrations will assist even the novice gardener to care for their rhododendrons and azaleas successfully. In this guide, Andrea Kögel, herself an expert in growing ornamental shrubs, imparts all the necessary information about propagating and caring for rhododendrons – from planting to fertilizing, from watering to pruning and winter protection. And, as even the best care cannot totally exclude the possibility of attack by pests and diseases, you will also find here all you need to know about their identification, prevention and control.

WARNING

Some rhododendron and azalea varieties contain toxic substances. Unfortunately, at present, no definite scientific information is available as to whether the concentration of toxins in these species and varieties is harmful to human health. One species that is definitely known to be toxic, however, is *Rhododendron luteum* (see p. 9). Please make sure that children and pets are not able to eat parts of this plant nor to come into contact with the nectar. As a precaution, always wash your hands after touching rhodendrons and azaleas.Some of the companion plants described on pages 58/59 are also toxic. These plants have been marked with the symbol ✿.

The flower of "Nova Zembla".

A modern rhododendron hybrid with beautiful, compact growth.

The author
Andrea Kögel is a trained gardener
and editor of the gardening
magazine *Mein Schöner Garten*.

Acknowledgements
The author and publishers wish to
thank rhododendron raiser Hans
Hachmann of Barmstedt (Germany)
for his expert advice.

An azalea showing autumn foliage.

All about rhododendrons and azaleas

Their magnificent, colourful blossom places rhododendrons and azaleas among the most beautiful ornamental garden shrubs. The following text gives a brief introduction to the classification and history of these splendid forest shrubs and a little information about the raising of cultivars and hybrids.

Rhododendrons belong to the botanical family of heather-like plants or *Ericaceae*. This very large family of plants is distributed all over the globe and contains approximately 2,000 different species. About half of these are rhododendrons. In the wild all *Ericaceae* grow on acid, humus-rich soils. This will give you some idea of the soil conditions required by rhododendrons in your garden. (Practical advice on checking your garden soil is given in the table on p. 13.) Unfortunately, at some time in the past somebody used the term "wetland plants" to describe rhododendrons, which resulted in less-experienced rhododendron enthusiasts planting their shrubs in wet ground, believing that this would suit them – with disastrous results – the reason for which is explained in the section on rhododendrons' countries of origin (see p. 10). Providing one does not plant them in marshy ground, however, these flowering shrubs are much easier to care for than is generally assumed. Once they have been planted in the right soil and in the right position, they will make very few demands with respect to care.

What is the difference between a rhododendron and an azalea?

Originally, botanists divided the genus *Rhododendron* into rhododendron species and azaleas. *The rhododendrons* once included mainly the evergreen species; *the azaleas* included the species which partly or completely lose their leaves in winter. However, in 1870 the Russian scientist Carl Maximowicz discovered that, in the strictist botanical sense, the two groups actually belong together. Since then, scientists have used only the name *Rhododendron* for this genus.

NB: Garden centres and nurseries have tended to continue to use the old terms and, even now, often make a distinction between rhododendrons and azaleas in their catalogues. For this reason, therefore, and whenever it seems sensible, we have also used the old names in this book.

From wild species to garden rhododendrons

Most rhododendrons that are planted in gardens today, or have been well established there for some time, are no longer pure wild species as found in nature. They are nearly always cultivars. The reason for this is that several of the wild species do not produce many flowers, flower irregularly, grow unattractively and look lanky, or cannot cope with the climate found in the temperate zones of the world. By comparison, rhododendrons that have been bred and cultivated are much more robust, as is shown by their profusion of flowers and colours, and often display a compact, bushy growth. Cultivars are created by crossing different species. In specialist language, they are called hybrids or varieties. Garden rhododendrons can be divided into seven distinct groups, depending on their origins, the way they grow and the shape of their flowers. The rhododendron enthusiast will come across these groups again and again, whether they are buying them in a garden centre or while browsing through a gardening catalogue. The table on page 6 will give you an initial introduction to these groups and their typical characteristics. Detailed descriptions and tips on their use in the garden or on a balcony or patio can be found on pages 17-33.

Japanese azaleas in full bloom
No other garden shrub can quite match this fiery colour display in late spring/early summer. In the foreground, the variety "Favorite"; left, the glowing red "Muttertag".

The major rhododendron groups

1. **Large-flowered hybrids:** large shrubs, generally over 1 m (40 in) tall, with large, leathery leaves and luxuriant, upright umbels. Countless varieties in many colours.
2. **Yakushimanum hybrids:** the shape of the flower is similar to that of the large-flowered varieties but, on the whole, they grow smaller and are very compact. Typical feature: shoots covered with a hairy, felt-like layer.
3. **Williamsianum hybrids:** grow in a compact, roundish shape, the leaves are round; flowers often pendent.
4. **Repens hybrids:** low-growing, spreading cushion shape, with rather open, red flowers.
5. **Wild varieties and their hybrids:** rhododendrons that have not, or have hardly been, tampered with by raisers; generally dwarf varieties with small flowers.
6. **Deciduous azaleas:** 1-2 m (40-80 in) tall shrubs with large flower umbels. They lose their leaves in winter.
7. **Japanese azaleas:** also known as evergreen azaleas, which lose some of their leaves in winter. Low, compact growth. Small flowers which bloom abundantly.

Rhododendrons for greenhouses and indoors

This is a group of rhododendrons that are sensitive to freezing temperatures and which cannot grow out of doors in a temperate climate but will ony thrive in a greenhouse or indoors.

● Tropical rhododendrons: most of these originate in the rainforests of Indonesia and flower all year round in the most beautiful, exotic colours. They are normally only found in greenhouses and botanical gardens as they are difficult to look after.
● Indoor azaleas: these are the azaleas you will see for sale in flowershops during winter and spring. Their correct botanical name is *Rhododendrum simsii* and their country of origin is China. Numerous varieties flower in shades of white, pink and red.

The botanical name

If you want to choose the right rhododendron for your needs and care for it properly, you will need to know its botanical name. Generally, the name consists of two Latin elements: the generic name and the species name.
Genus: This is the first name and is always capitalized.
Example: *Rhododendron* (translation: *rhodon* – rose and *dendron* – tree, which yields "rose tree").
Species name: This name is the second one and supplies information on the plant's typical characteristics, its country of origin and sometimes the name of the person who discovered it.
Example: *yakushimanum* – originating from the island of Yaku Shima. The name of the plant is, therefore, *Rhododendron yakushimanum* or, abbreviated, *R. yakushimanum*.
Variety name: Very often, there is a third name, the name of the variety. This is the name of the cultivar and it is always placed in quotation marks. Example: *Rhododendron yakushimanum* "Barmstedt". Variety names are often quite imaginative. They can range from names of towns or cities to names of famous personalities or even such evocative names as "Azurwolke" (Azure Cloud) or "Morning Magic".
NB: If certain cultivars can no longer definitely be assigned to one species or another because of their complicated background, the species name is dropped and the name will be given as, for example, *Rhododendron* "Praecox" or simply *R.* "Praecox". This happens rather often in the huge group of large-flowered rhododendron hybrids.

Shapes of flowers

1. *Large-flowered hybrid with very large, single flowers and a dome-shaped, very compact cluster of flowers. 2. Yakushimanum hybrid with large flowers in compact, rounded umbels. 3. Williamsianum hybrids – the large, bell-shaped flower clusters often lean gracefully to one side, forming open umbels.*

Shapes of growth

You will no doubt have seen plenty of bushy rhododendrons in gardens or in public parks. They can be large or small, round, funnel-shaped or upright. In temperate climates, for example, their dimensions may reach truly gigantic proportions, with huge thickets of rhododendrons extending along roads or through woods. In their countries of origin, they can develop into veritable trees, growing up to heights of 12 m (39 ft) and more. *R. giganteum*, the giant rhododendron, is reputed to grow to a height of up to 30 m (98 ft)! Some of the big species can live for several hundred years. At the other end of the scale, there are little dwarfs with a cushion-like growth, such as *R. keleticum*, which just manages to grow a few centimetres high. These small, flat-growing species often originate from mountainous areas or sub-polar regions where they may be covered with a thick blanket of snow for a good part of the year.

How quickly do rhododendrons grow?

The speed of growth will depend entirely on the group to which each rhododendron belongs. The large-flowered hybrids grow fastest: they can increase by 20 cm (8 in) or more per year! Repens hybrids and Japanese azaleas, however, can only produce about 5 cm (2 in) of new growth each year.
General rule: The lower the final height, the slower the growth.

Rhododendron roots

Roots are designed to absorb water and nutrients and to anchor the plant in the surrounding soil. The roots can also tell us something about the plant's natural habitat which, in turn, tells us something about its requirements in regard to care. Rhododendrons usually grow on rocky ground or mountain slopes in their countries of origin; some tropical species are even epiphytes (which means that they grow on other plants but can nourish themselves independently by drawing moisture from the air). In the wild, even when rooted in the ground, these tropical shrubs usually have only a thin layer of humus at their disposal. For this reason, over the course of time, they have developed a widely branching, very flat and spreading root system through which they can absorb vital nutrients from the surface layers of the soil. This has proved an advantage as rhododendrons are thus easy to transplant because of their shallow rooting system. On the other hand, they may also dry out rather easily because their roots cannot penetrate into the deeper levels of the soil, so they need a regular supply of water.

The flowers

Rhododendrons attract attention even from a distance with their magnificent flowers. What you are looking at, however, is not an individual flower but entire flower umbels or clusters of flowers. These umbels, consisting of several flowerheads, can be pipe-shaped, funnel-shaped, bell-shaped or dish-shaped. The classic form is the upright, compact umbel which is most clearly seen among the large-flowered hybrids and the Yakushimanum hybrids, whereas the flowers of other species may turn sideways or hang down gracefully, for example, *Rhododendron williamsianum*. The individual flower consists of five to seven petals that have merged together. Five to sixteen stamens are equipped with rather sticky pollen. The ovary contains five to twenty compartments. Pollination is carried out by honey bees or bumble bees.

Flower colours

When it comes to colours, probably only the rose can match rhododendrons with its variety of different shades. Almost any colour you can think of will be found among the rhododendrons; there are even some dual-coloured varieties or varieties with different-coloured markings. Among the large-flowered hybrids the dominant colours are shades of pink, purple, violet and white, while the deciduous azaleas more often appear in shades of yellow and orange.

4. Repens hybrid with bell-shaped flowers that hang down gracefully.
5. Wild species with rather small flowers which may form open or dense umbels, depending on the species. 6. Deciduous azaleas with large, individual flowers in dome-shaped umbels. 7. Japanese azaleas with small, densely clustered flowers.

Flowering time

If you utilize the entire range of species available, you can manage to have flowering rhododendrons in your garden for four months of the year. In some places, the variety R. "Praecox" will bloom as early as the first month of spring. The last species to flower, at the end of the first month of summer and the beginning of the second, are a few large-flowered hybrids derived from R. discolor. The main flowering time for rhododendrons, however, is in the last month of spring and the first month of summer. Around this time, the colours of a rhododendron garden will resemble a great burst of fireworks.

Scented rhododendrons

As a rule, rhododendrons are not fragrant but there are some notable exceptions. One of these is R. fortunei, an attractive, hardy, wild species with large, porcelain-white flowers, and also its cultivars, the large-flowered hybrids "Bellfontaine" and "Direktor E. Hjelm".

The most exciting scent is probably that of the Ponticum azalea (Rhododendron luteum). On sunny days one single shrub may envelop an entire garden in a sweet, heady cloud of fragrance.

Warning: The Ponticum azalea is toxic (all parts of the plant)!

The leaves

Most rhododendrons are evergreen. Only the deciduous azaleas and some Arctic and Alpine rhododendron species lose their leaves in

A decorative shrub in a large container

R. impeditum "Azurwolke" attracts attention with its brilliantly coloured flowers. It prefers a semi-sunny position.

winter or early spring. The Japanese azaleas lose only some of their foliage.

The shapes and sizes of leaves show a huge range of variations, from narrow, spear-shaped leaves to almost completely round leaves, in sizes ranging from barely a centimetre (less than ½ in) (R. intricatum) to 1 m (40 in) long in one subtropical species.

The colour of the leaves also demonstrates an astonishing array of possibilities, particularly among the new shoots in spring. R. williamsianum and its hybrids, for example, produce red or copper-coloured shoots, while R. yakushimanum has conspicuous young shoots that are covered in white, felty hairs. Many azaleas produce breathtakingly beautiful colours in autumn, ranging from wine red to orange-yellow.

The leaves of rhododendrons are like calling cards for the botanist. The shape, size and, in particular, any hairiness or scales on the undersides of the leaves give points of reference when determining the species.

The countries of origin of rhododendrons

With the exception of the African continent, rhododendrons are distributed across the entire northern hemisphere of the globe. South-East Asia, which is home to the tropical species of rhododendrons, is the only place where they are occasionally to be found south of the equator. One single species is known in Australia. Western and central China and the Himalayas together make up the region that is a natural paradise for rhododendrons. No other place on earth has so many different species. Here one will find rhododendrons in subtropical jungle valleys as well as in

the more elevated, wet, cool mountain forests and on bare, rocky slopes up to altitudes of 5,000 m (16,400 ft).

Other major areas of distribution are North America and Japan. Finally, Europe has no fewer than nine wild species, among them the well-known Alpine species of R. ferrugineum and R. hirsutum.

How rhododendrons were discovered

Plant hunters first transported rhododendrons during the eighteenth and nineteenth centuries, as was the case with so many other garden plants. As early as the seventeenth century, however, there were reports from Japan of beautiful azaleas, but political conditions made it impossible to import plants to Europe until much later. In the meantime, collectors had been bringing back a number of important rhododendron species from North America and Asia Minor. Like the Japanese, the Chinese also tended to close their country to foreign visitors and so the veritable "treasure house" of the Himalayas could only be guessed at until 1820. The British were particularly enthusiastic. Sir Joseph Dalton Hooker – the director of the Royal Botanic Gardens at Kew – brought home 43 new rhododendron species alone. A second great wave of imports, around 1900-30, brought several hundred more species to Europe. Finding the most remote homes of rhododendrons often meant travelling, mainly on foot, for weeks, even months. Neither the climate nor the wild animals showed much consideration for the rhododendron fever that had gripped Europe, and native tribespeople did not welcome the intruders either, so many a collector literally risked life and limb in pursuit of his desire.

Preparations for planting

If the soil, the position and the climate are right, rhododendrons will prove totally uncomplicated flowering shrubs. However, even if the conditions are less than favourable, you need not give up hope of such flowering splendour in your garden. A few adjustments will provide your plants with a comfortable environment in which to thrive.

The main prerequisite: the right position

In order to decide on this, one must consider all the factors in the environment which have a direct bearing on the growth of a plant. These will include the acidity and consistency of the soil and humidity and light conditions, as well as the prevailing direction and strength of the wind.

In their native homes, most rhododendrons grow in mountainous areas and in cool, damp mountain forests. Here, mist and rain will always combine to provide the air and soil with a high level of moisture. As the terrain is generally sloping, water always drains away quickly so there is never any waterlogging. Like most humus-rich soils, a typical forest soil will be fairly acidic. The more the conditions in your garden approximate those of your chosen rhododendrons' natural habitats, the more your rhododendrons will feel at home.

Finding the right position

If you wish to plant rhododendrons in your garden, you should check the following points:

- soil acidity (see below);
- type of soil (see p. 12);
- degree of moisture in the soil (see p. 15);
- air humidity (see p. 15);
- conditions of light (see p. 15);
- prevailing direction and strength of the wind (see p. 16).

Soil acidity

Rhododendrons grow best in acid soil with a pH factor somewhere between 4.5 and 5.8. If the rhododendron has been grafted on to a robust base species (see p. 55), it may be able to cope with a pH factor of 6.5. The pH factor of most cultivated gardens is usually somewhere between 5 and 8, so, sometimes, the soil might be too alkaline for rhododendrons.

pH factor

The pH factor (from Latin *potentia hydrogenii* – potency of water) defines the whole range of chemical reactions, from acid to alkaline, in the soil on a scale of 1-14. Factor 7 is a neutral reaction of the soil. Factors below this are more or less acid; factors above 7 indicate alkaline soil. The pH factor is largely determined by the chalk or lime content in the soil. The more chalk there is in the soil, the higher the pH factor will register, which means the lower the acid content will be.

How to determine the pH value

A slightly acidic soil is the determining factor for the well-being of rhododendrons. If you are planting them for the first time, you should definitely test your soil first. Various testers are available in the gardening trade, so you will be able to determine your own garden's pH factor quite easily.

- Take a handful of soil from six different spots in the place where you intend to plant your rhododendrons.
- Mix the samples together thoroughly.
- Pour distilled water on to approximately 1 tsp of this mixture.
- Use an indicator strip and the colour scale supplied with your soil tester to determine the pH factor. If you want a really exact reading, you can send your samples to a soil research institute, where the factor will be determined to a very exact degree. You can obtain the address of such a place from your local garden centre.

A garden pond is a particularly favourable setting for showing off your rhododendron shrubs.

As described above, take soil samples from six different spots, mix them, put them in a plastic bag and send them to the soil institute.

My tip: Although it is a great deal more expensive, another way to test the pH of your soil is with a pH meter, obtainable in the gardening trade. You simply push this into the soil and, after a few seconds, you will be able to read the result.

How to lower the pH factor

The best way to lower the pH factor is by working peat into the soil. If you would like to lower the pH factor by one point, for example from 6.5 to 5.5, you would have to reckon on about six bales of moist peat worked in to a depth of 30 cm (12 in) over an area of 10 sq m (12 sq yd).

How to raise the pH factor

Use lime to raise the pH factor. To raise the factor by one point on the scale (for example, from 3.5 to 4.5), sprinkle the following amounts of lime on 10 sq m (12 sq yd):

- on a light soil, 1.5 kg (3.3 lb) grey lime or 3 kg (6.6 lb) grey calcium carbonate;
- on a medium-heavy soil, 2.5 kg (5.5 lb) grey slag lime;
- on heavy soil, 3 kg (6.6 lb) grey slag lime.

What happens if the pH factor is incorrect?

If the pH factor is too high, plants which are accustomed to acid soils can no longer absorb iron or magnesium, both of which are essential for the formation of chlorophyll.

"Schneegold" has brilliant white flowers with yellow centres.

The result will be yellowing leaves, which may show green veins to begin with, followed by a complete cessation of growth in the entire plant. The higher the pH factor stands above 7, the more visible these symptoms of deficiency will become. This condition is called chlorosis (see p. 49). If the pH factor is too low (below 4), on the other hand, the roots will be damaged. The plant will not develop new roots and will eventually be unable to absorb nutrients.

The importance of humus

The ideal soil for rhododendrons is loose, aerated soil which can store sufficient moisture without becoming waterlogged and which provides all the essential nutrients for the plants. Humus represents a veritable elixir of life to rhododendrons. If your soil is poor in humus, you must raise the humus content (see p. 13). Humus is produced by the action of soil bacteria and other micro-organisms on organic components in the soil. It improves the structure of the soil, stores nutrients and moisture and, because of its porous nature, maintains the soil in a loose, well-aerated condition. Humic acid, which is created by the decomposition of humus, plays a vital role in breaking down the nutrients that are essential for plant growth. The best provider of humus is compost, but dead leaves, wood chips, composted bark, sawdust, peat, horn meal and dried blood, as well as all animal manures, are suitable.

"Indicator" plants

"Indicator" plants can be a great help in determining the nature of the soil in your garden. These are wild plants that show a preference for particular soils. Their presence will give you a first indication as to the make-up of your soil. The more samples of a particular indicator plant you find in a particular spot, the more certain you can be about the type of soil you are dealing with. These "green indicators" do not offer an absolute guarantee, however, as many wild plants are surprisingly adaptable and will thrive on soils other than those they are supposed to prefer. These plants will often arrive in your garden as "stowaways" in pot plants and rootstocks bought from a garden centre or nursery.

The table shown on the right lists the most important types of soils and will tell you which indicator plants are symptomatic of certain soils. If you are not familiar with the indicator plants mentioned here, you will be able to find out more about them by referring to a good plant guide. Many indicator plants are better known as weeds!

How to identify soils and improve them

Humus-rich soil

Comprises mainly decomposed leaves, wood or peat. If your garden is situated on a site formerly occupied by forest, or on reclaimed marshland, or has large stands of trees or shrubs, you may may be dealing with humus-rich soil.

Characteristics:
● loose structure;
● the ability to store moisture;
● usually, a low pH factor.
Indicator plants: bracken (*Pteridium aquilinum*), sheep's sorrel (*Rumex acetosella*), wild violets or pansies (*Viola spp.*), heather (*Erica spp.*).

Soil improvement: usually not necessary, but check to make sure that the pH factor is not too low.

Light, sandy soil

Dries out quickly in summer and can be worked with ease all the year round.

Characteristics:
● loose structure;
● good water permeability;
● usually, a low pH factor;
Indicator plants: *Crocosmia spp., Centaurea spp., Lupinus spp., Viscaria vulgaris.*

Soil improvement: bark compost, leaf mould, peat or other organic matter, worked in well. This will improve the soil's ability to store water and nutrients.

Heavy loam and clay soils

Usually an above-average nutrient content, but badly aerated and having a tendency to become too dense. After a heavy rain shower, water tends to lie on the surface for several hours.

Characteristics:
● stickiness and fine structure;
● usually, a high pH factor;
● poor air and water permeability;
Indicator plants: creeping buttercup (*Ranunculus repens*); dandelion (*Taraxacum officinale*); lesser celandine (*Ranunculus ficaria*); comfrey (*Symphytum officinale*).

Soil improvement: mixing in plenty of sand, coarsely chopped wood shavings, bark compost, peat and other organic matter will help.

Agricultural soil, sandy, humus-rich soil

The right balance between loamy, sandy and humus-rich soil.

Characteristics:
● crumbly texture;
● fairly good water permeability;
● middle-range pH factor;
Indicator plants: common nettle (*Urtica dioica*), and small nettle (*U. urens*), gallant soldier (*Galinsoga parviflora*), common orache (*Atriplex patula*), chickweed (*Stellaria media*).

Soil improvement: dig out the area to be planted and mix the soil in a ratio of 1:1 with peat or leaf compost.

Chalky soil

Warms up quickly, dries out easily and provides most unfavourable conditions for rhododendrons.

Characteristics:
● loose structure;
● high degree of water permeability;
● high pH factor (over 8).
Indicator plants: chicory (*Cichorium intybus*), meadow clary (*Salvia pratensis*), wall germander (*Teucrium chamaedrys*), forking larkspur (*Consolida regalis*).

Soil improvement: hardly possible for rhododendrons. Exchange of soil recommended or build a raised bed (see p. 14).

Totally unfavourable conditions

If soil conditions are extremely unfavourable for rhododendrons, simply improving the structure of the soil will not be sufficient. This is particularly the case:

● if the subsoil is very dense or impermeable to water (waterlogging);

● if the ground water level is high;

● on chalky soil with a pH factor of over 8;

● on extremely heavy soil (pure clay).

If you have these conditions and still wish to grow rhododendrons, there are three possible methods:

1. Exchanging the soil.

2. Raising an existing flowerbed containing the right kind of soil.

3. Building a raised bed from scratch.

In all three cases you will require large quantities of suitable soil. You can mix suitable soil for rhododendrons yourself or buy it in the gardening trade.

Mixing your own rhododendron soil: All the ingredients should be well moistened to begin with and then mixed thoroughly.

You will need:

2 bales of ordinary garden peat;

1 wheelbarrow load of two-year-old compost, consisting of chopped pine or fir branches, bark or dead leaves;

half a wheelbarrow load of coarse sand;

4 handfuls of horn chips.

Bought soil: Special fertilized peat for rhododendrons mixed with ordinary peat in a ratio of 1:1. Mix well and moisten.

Exchanging the soil

Dig out a pit for planting the rhododendrons. For smaller rhododendrons and dwarf rhododendrons, the pit should be 30-40 cm (12-16 in) deep, for taller varieties 40-60 cm (16-24 in) deep, and the diameter of the pit should be three times the size of the rootstock. Fill the pit with the prepared or bought rhododendron soil.

NB: If the soil is very chalky, line the walls of the pit (but never the bottom) with polythene, so that water containing chalk cannot soak into the sides of the pit. Line the floor of the pit with a 10-cm (4 in) layer of fir tree branches, chopped wood or pieces of bark. This will prevent water from rising up from below.

My tip: Use the empty peat sacks for lining the walls of the pit. If a sack is cut open, one will suffice for two small shrubs.

Raising a flowerbed

If there is a tendency to waterlogging and dense subsoil, an exchange of soil will be necessary. I recommend raising an entire flowerbed for several shrubs instead of digging individual planting pits (see illustration below).

NB: If the subsoil has a very high chalk content, especially on slopes, line the walls of the bed with polythene sheeting, so that water with a high chalk content cannot penetrate the bed. Cover the floor of the bed with a 10-cm (4 in) layer of coarsely chopped wood or bark or with conifer branches. This will prevent water rising up from below.

A raised bed

Digging a pit can be avoided if you build a raised bed, although you will need approximately one-third more soil for building up the bed. On the other hand, a raised bed can be built even on a hard surface like asphalt or concrete. The best idea is to build a bed that will accommodate several rhododendrons right from the start.

As long as the soil has not become completely hard, roughly dig over the planting area beforehand. Then set the boundaries of your planting area with wooden planks, pieces of tree trunk, old railway sleepers, lime-free chunks of rock, stones or a wooden palisade. The frame of the bed should be at least 50-60 cm (20-24 in) high. Fill the bed with suitable rhododendron soil.

Raising an existing flowerbed

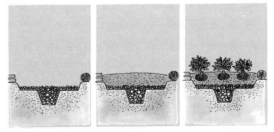

Remove a 40-cm (16 in) layer of soil from the area of the flowerbed, then dig over the bottom of the bed and dig a 30-cm (12 in) deep trench along the entire length of it. Fill the trench with gravel and the bottom of the bed with a 20-cm (8 in) layer of coarse sand, gravel or chopped conifer branches. Finally, fill the bed with a 30-40-cm (12-16 in) layer of soil.

Building a raised bed
Define the planting area with wooden planks, loosely piled stones or tree trunks up to a height of 50-60 cm (20-24 in) and fill the bed with rhododendron soil.

Moisture in the soil
When choosing a position for planting your rhododendrons, consider how much moisture is available in the soil. Too much can be just as harmful as too little.

Rhododendrons do not like wet soil
In the past there has been a tendency for gardeners to believe they are doing their rhododendrons a good turn by planting them in a very moist or even boggy position. The person who first suggested such marshy conditions was probably thinking more of the low pH factor and high humus content of soil in marshy areas than of an abundance of moisture but the type of waterlogged soil that is typical of marshland or moorland is bad for rhododendrons. Waterlogging usually occurs if the subsoil is hard or dense. Sometimes, a water-impermeable layer in the subsoil, like rock or clay, may prevent water from draining away.

Symptoms of waterlogging or too much moisture: Water lying in puddles hours after rainfall, extensive growth of mosses or green algae on the surface of the soil.

How to remedy waterlogging:
● In less severe cases, a thorough loosening of the soil will often be sufficient; dig over the soil to two spade-depths down.
● Work in plenty of loose matter: chopped wood or bark, sawdust, compost, coarse sand, straw or dead leaves.
● Fill the planting pit with a drainage layer (10 cm or 4 in) of chopped wood or coarse sand.
● In severe cases, lay drainage pipes or raise the bed itself (raising a flowerbed, building a raised bed, see p. 14).

Humidity
Even if rhododendrons do not like consistently wet feet, they love plenty of moist air. Rhododendrons will grow particularly well in regions with a maritime climate (for example, in Britain or northern Germany). In the garden humidity can be raised by planting trees and shrubs, by having a good cover of plants from the leaves of which water is constantly evaporating or by having expanses of water, like streams or garden ponds. On warm, dry days, you should employ a sprinkler or garden hose; a mere five minutes of spraying in the morning and evening will do.

Light conditions
As rhododendrons are forest- or forest-edge-dwelling plants, most species prefer semi-shade or light similar to that in a forest glade, but not complete shade. If they have too little light, they will not flower nearly as well. Too much sunlight, on the other hand, will lead to excessive evaporation and the result will often be damage through dryness, particularly if it is coupled with low humidity and high temperatures. Overexposure to sunlight will also cause the flowering time to be over too quickly.

General rule: The cooler the climate, and the higher the humidity in the air, the sunnier should be the ideal position for your rhododendrons! Deciduous azaleas and Japanese azaleas, small-leaved dwarf rhododendrons and Yakushimanum hybrids usually need more sunlight than the other groups of rhododendrons.

Shade providers
Taller trees and shrubs will naturally provide some shade. All deep-rooted species with open crowns, like pines, oaks, ginko, acacia, hawthorn, laburnum, magnolia and *Liquidambar spp.* are especially suitable.
Shallow-rooting trees and trees with dense foliage are not suitable as they will prevent rain from reaching the rhododendron shrubs and their shallow roots will compete with the flat-rooting rhododendrons. Among the latter types are birch, maple, beech, chestnut, fir and linden trees. Do not plant rhododendrons under any of these trees. If you have no other alternative, you could always build a raised bed.

Planting beneath trees
Deep-rooting tree species are no problem in combination with rhododendrons. In contrast, rhododendrons should be planted well away from the roots of shallow-rooting trees, or in a raised bed.

An enchanting grove of rhododendrons, Japanese azaleas, ferns and ornamental shrubs.

My tip: Suitable places to plant rhododendrons can be found in the shade of buildings, provided the spot is draught-free. West-facing walls are ideal as they benefit from late-afternoon sun, but wind-sheltered north- or east-facing walls are suitable too.

Check the prevailing wind

Rhododendrons do like a position with plenty of fresh air but are not happy if they are exposed to wind all of the time. Draughts and permanent breezes from a north-easterly direction are very bad for rhododendrons. Such conditions will dry out the shrubs and cause the lower parts of the branches to become bare. Sharp winds in winter are particularly bad as then frozen soil may prevent the roots from drawing in moisture. Dense planting of deciduous trees or conifers, a high hedge or house walls and solid fences will provide the best protection from wind. Corners of houses, spaces between buildings and unprotected areas, particularly on south- or west-facing slopes, are often too draughty and should be avoided. If rhododendrons have already been planted there, consider transplanting them!

A selection of beautiful rhododendrons

The following pages offer a few examples from the huge selection of available rhododendron varieties and hybrids. This selection is intended to give you an impression of the multitude of shapes and colours to be found.

This chapter offers a representative cross-section from the several thousand rhododendron cultivars found worldwide. In addition to well-tried favourites, you will be introduced to some brand new cultivars and a few rarities. The typical characteristics of the various rhododendron groups, plant descriptions and relevant information will make it easier for you to choose rhododendrons in your favourite colours for your type of garden, patio, border or balcony. The rhododendrons shown here are divided into seven groups, depending on their origins and appearance. As a rule, most tree nurseries and garden centres abide by this classification system. Essential basic information is provided by the table on page 6. The most important characteristics of each group are given first and you will also be given interesting details on the shape of growth, flowering times, colours of flowers and the most suitable uses for each group. Often, I have indicated rhododendrons with special characteristics,

such as very flat-rooting cultivars, and varieties that are recommended for their beautiful flowers and particularly decorative young shoots. These recommendations of certain species are intended to help you to identify rhododendrons to suit your requirements among the confusingly large range of varieties on the market.

Plant descriptions

Descriptions of group characteristics are accompanied by photographs of rhododendron varieties and an outline of their main features. Naturally, I am only able to give a small cross-section from the huge range in existence but I hope you will find plenty of inspiration and advice to meet your requirements and suit the conditions in your garden.

Flowering times and colours

This information will be found in the flowering calendar on pages 34/35. This contains a selection of well-tried and promising new varieties, chosen by rhododendron experts

and gardeners, and arranged according to colour and flowering times.

Once you have some idea of the many varieties available, you will be able to work out an ideal selection. You will soon find that it is not just a matter of choosing and planting any rhododendron variety. You will need to harmonize the colours of those shrubs with simultaneous flowering times in order to obtain the best effect. If your aim is to have a long period of continuous flowering, you must choose plants with different flowering times.

The best rhododendron for each site

The best choice of plant for a particular site or purpose will be made after studying the group descriptions. A quick overview may be given as follows:

Rhododendrons for larger gardens: vigorously growing, large-flowered hybrids, deciduous azaleas.

For small gardens: Yakushimanum hybrids, Williamsianum hybrids and Repens hybrids; Japanese azaleas; slow-growing, large-flowered hybrids.For sunny positions: deciduous azaleas, Yakushimanum hybrids; wild species and their hybrids.

For large containers: Yakushimanum hybrids, Williamsianum hybrids, Repens hybrids; Japanese azaleas.

For pots and balcony boxes: low-growing wild species and their hybrids; Diamant azaleas (Japanese azaleas).

For high hedgerows/borders (as a screen): large-flowered hybrids. For front gardens: Repens hybrids; Yakushimanum hybrids.

For rockeries: wild species and their hybrids; Repens hybrids; Diamant azaleas (Japanese azaleas).

For beautiful autumn colours: Japanese azaleas; deciduous azaleas.

Rhododendrons as cut flowers

In northern Germany, which has a maritime climate and where rhodo-dendrons flourish particularly well, a charming custom is practised. As soon as the first rhododendron buds begin to open, a few vigorous branches will be cut from the shrub and placed in a large jug or vase on the doorstep, as a greeting to visitors. If you have only one or two rhododendron shrubs in your garden, this would, of course, be rather a waste of your precious blooms. Nevertheless, one some-times finds an odd branch that is in the way or sticks out untidily, which can be cut off and used for such a vase arrangement. Cut the branch when the flowers are just on the point of opening, make a slit of 2-3 cm (1-1¼ in) at the end of the stem and spray the leaves and flowers daily with water. This will ensure that your splendid display will last for at least a week. Of course, a handsome flowering plant like this also merits a special place in your living room. The almost voluptuous umbels are especially effective if placed in front of a mirror, for example. Individual flowers can also be floated on the surface of a flat dish filled with water.

Perfect harmony
Colours that have been chosen to blend harmoniously will make a breathtaking picture: here, the varieties: "Catharine van Tol", "Catawbiense Boursault" and "Blue Peter". They would also look extremely elegant as cut flowers in a vase.

18

Large-flowered hybrids

The large-flowered rhododendron hybrids grow into 1-5-m (40-200 in) tall shrubs that spread out and sometimes develop almost a funnel shape; they grow upright and have fairly large, shiny green leaves. The luxuriant, slightly domed flower umbels have a diameter of up to 15 cm (6 in). There is a huge selection of varieties, in colours ranging from white to red and pink to deepest

A hedge consisting entirely of rhododendrons and azaleas.

violet. There is also an ever-increasing range of yellow, orange and salmon pink flowering cultivars on offer. Varieties that have flowers with an "eye" (a conspicuous light or dark centre), which gives them an almost orchid-like beauty, are particularly popular.

"Lee's Dark Purple", an old, very popular variety, is conspicuous for the attractive yellow and green markings on its flowers. The shrub is spreading and upright in habit.

"Sappho", which was bred in Britain during the last century, still enchants the onlooker with the exotic appearance of its white flowers bearing startling dark centres. Unfortunately, this variety is rather sensitive to frost. In regions with an unsympathetic climate, you should grow instead the very similar but far more robust variety "Schneebukett" (Snow Bouquet).

"Purple Splendour" is considered to be one of the most beautiful violet varieties. Its flowers appear particularly dark because of their almost black centres with white stamens. It grows upright and fairly open and requires a sheltered position.

"Furnivall's Daughter" (Raiser: Knap Hill, Britain) – nearly all rhododendron enthusiasts love this variety with its giant, orchid-like flowers. Each individual flower may have a diameter of up to 10 cm (4 in). This variety tends to grow outward rather than upward and can be highly recommended as a plant for large containers. Unfortunately, it is only suitable for sheltered positions as it is sensitive to frost.

"Dr H. C. Dresselhuys" was raised in the Netherlands in 1920 and is still one of the most reliable standard varieties with vigorous, upright growth. The compact cluster of flowers is extremely beautiful

"Album Novum" grows vigorously and upright. The compact flower umbels are tinted pale lilac to begin with, then turn white. A well-proven variety for larger gardens.

"Brasilia" is one of the most exciting and unusual new introductions of the last few years. The almost tropical-looking, tri-coloured flowers bloom in dense, compact clusters as early as the last month of spring.

"Catawbiense Boursault", raised over a hundred years ago in France, is impressive for its robust good health and vigorous growth. It looks best in spacious gardens under high trees.

"Hachmann's Feuerschein". Rhododendron raiser Hans Hachmann caused a sensation in the red range of cultivars with this new hybrid. It is characterized by late, brilliant cherry red flowers, which retain the intensity of their colour from the moment they open until they fade. The shrub is low-growing and starts flowering profusely while it is still a young plant.

"Nova Zembla" is the most common red among the vigorously growing varieties. In addition to 14-cm (5½ in) diameter flowers with violet-brown markings in the centre, it also possesses conspicuous, attractive, dark green foliage.

"Memoir", is a hybrid that was cultivated by A. Waterer in Britain in 1911 and was rediscovered recently. It bears extremely beautiful white flowers that are tinged with a delicate shade of violet when they open and have a noticeable golden green centre. Its foliage is particularly attractive all year round, being a fresh shade of green. It grows low and has an attractive shape. This variety is particularly hardy.

"Viscy" (Raiser: Dietrich G. Hobbie) is very decorative with its large, individual flowers in an unusual shade of amber. Unfortunately, this variety is somewhat sensitive to frost. As it is an early flowering shrub with an extremely long flowering time (up to three weeks), it is definitely worth attempting to grow it in your garden.

In time, the large-flowered hybrids will grow into veritable mountains of flowers.

Flowering splendour in late spring and early summer

The main flowering time of the large-flowered rhododendron hybrids is from late spring into early summer. In the last month of spring, the shrubs are transformed into veritable mountains of flowers. A few varieties, like "Canary" and "Jacksonii", will begin to flower as early as the end of the second month of spring; others, like "Album Nova" and "Hachmann's Feuerschein", do not flower until well into the first month of summer. When choosing varieties for your garden, consider the speed of growth of the individual varieties as well as their flowering time and colour. Whereas many older culti-vars can become rather large, many of the newer varieties are much smaller and lower.

Use large-flowered rhododendron hybrids individually or in groups. They are very suitable for creating a background in a shady shrubbery. Some varieties are also suitable as a hedge or as a large container plant.

Yakushimanum hybrids

The Yakushimanum hybrids are a relatively new group of garden rhododendrons which appeared on the market for the first time during the 1970s. At first glance, they look similar to the large-flowered hybrids but the growth of these shrubs is considerably smaller and more compact. Depending on the variety, they will rarely grow taller than 80 cm (32 in), even when mature, but will spread up to twice as wide as their height. Even very young plants will produce an abundance of white, pink and red flowers during the last month of spring/first month of summer. A typical feature of this group is the colour changes that the flowers undergo from the moment the buds open until they fade. The most obvious example of this colour change is the wild species *Rhododendron yakushimanum*, which is the ancient ancestor of the whole group. Its flowers are deep pink when in bud, turn light pink as they open and are white when in full bloom. A further unmistakable feature of this rhododendron type is a white, felt-like layer that appears on the young shoots in early summer. This is not, as some rhododendron owners are inclined to think, the beginnings of a pest infestation or some disease but a natural reaction by the plant to prevent its sensitive young shoots from losing moisture through evaporation. From the point of view of decorative value, these conspicuously light-coloured shoot tips are a plus as they stand out attractively against the older, dark green foliage.

"Daniela" is an extremely prostrate-growing shrub which has pretty, distinctive, light green foliage. The bright red flowers, which grow in dense, 11-13-cm (4¼-5 in) wide umbels, have much lighter centres, so this really can be described as a multi-coloured variety.

When in full bloom "Schneekrone" looks like a frilly cushion. At first the flowers are tinged the most delicate shade of pink and then turn completely white when they are fully opened. The petals have attractive wavy edges. The umbels may be up to 11 cm (4¼ in) across.

Yakushimanum hybrids can tolerate, indeed they require, more sunshine than most other rhododendrons. They are almost universally suitable for planting in the garden, providing the soil has been properly prepared: for example, in a spring flowerbed, as an early planting or underplanting, together with large-flowered rhododendron hybrids, in a rockery and, naturally, as a large container plant on a balcony or patio. It is a good idea to group several young plants of the same colour close together right from the start. Later, when the shrubs have grown, they can be moved quite easily.

"Babette" is a beautiful shade of champagne pink when the flowers begin to open; later they turn light yellow with a glowing red spot at the centre of each flower. This variety forms dense, roundish shrubs. A ten-year-old plant will grow no taller than 90 cm (36 in) and no wider than 130 cm (52 in).

Rhododendron yakushimanum, the wild ancestor of the Yakushimanum hybrids, grows silvery-white, felty shoots which continue to form an attractive feature for weeks after the flowering period is over. Unfortunately, the hybrids do not demonstrate this feature to quite the same extent.

"Koichiro Wada" is an extremely attractive cultivar of Rhododendron yakushimanum, in which the features of the wild species have been retained: the flowers pass through a series of colour changes, the leaves are dark-coloured, leathery and convex and the shrub grows in a cushion shape.

25

Williamsianum hybrids

Early flowering, compact growth and decorative foliage are advantageous features of these rhododendron hybrids which were raised by crossing the Chinese wild species *Rhododendron williamsianum* and large-flowered species. Depending on the variety, they may grow 1-2 m (40-80 in) tall. They grow very slowly and form densely foliated, round bushes. The large flowers are arranged in loose umbels and often lean gracefully to one side.

The flowering time is from late in the second month of spring to the end of spring. This means that Williamsianum hybrids flower exactly in the time slot that exists between the very early-flowering Repens hybrids and the large-flowered rhododendron hybrids. The comparatively small range of varieties includes many colours from red, pink, pale violet and creamy yellow shades to pure white. After the flowering time is over, their very attractive, rounded leaves and the chestnut-coloured new shoots of some varieties will continue to draw the eye. The varieties "Gartendirektor Glocker", "Lissabon" and "Stadt Essen" are particularly conspicuous in this respect. During autumn and winter, wine red flowerbuds provide an additional, attractive feature. Williamsianum hybrids are just made for growing in large containers. In the garden, they can be planted in front of taller rhododendron varieties and will also look good in a front garden or in a semi-shady rockery.

"Stadt Essen". Beautiful reddish-pink flowers with lighter centres in luxuriant umbels almost completely cover this broad, upright shrub from as early as the beginning of the third month of spring. Later, bronze-coloured, young shoots, dispersed all over the dark green foliage, are an eye-catching feature.

"Gartendirektor Glocker". A popular, very dense, slow-growing variety with beautiful, roundish leaves which are a remarkable bronze colour while they are shooting. The pink flowers have lighter centres.

"Gartendirektor Rieger" is a particularly beautiful creamy white variety. The edges of the flower petals are slightly wavy and have unusual wine red spots in their centres. Brownish-red buds stand out amid the foliage during the winter. Ten-year-old shrubs can grow as tall as 1-1.2 m (40-48 in) and about 1.4 m (56 in) wide.

**A profusion of flowers
from mid-spring onwards**

Repens hybrids

The desire of many owners of small gardens – small, early-flowering rhododendrons, requiring little space and beginning their flowering season very early – was met in the 1950s and 1960s with the large-scale introduction of Repens hybrids. The source of these new rhododendron varieties was the wild species of *Rhododendron repens*, originating in Tibet and China, a small shrub with creeping growth and early, glowing-red, bell-shaped flowers. By crossing these species with various other rhododendron species and garden hybrids, the well-known rhododendron raiser Dietrich G. Hobbie was able to develop these valuable dwarf rhododendrons which are no taller than 0.75-1.20 m (30-48 in) when fully grown, but which can grow as wide as 1-2 m (40-80 in). Umbels, consisting of three to seven hanging, bell-shaped flowers, open as early as the beginning of the second month of spring (depending on the weather) and follow the flowering of the first few early wild varieties to provide a fitting overture to the rhododendron flowering season. These varieties differ only slightly in colour. Nearly all of them are light to dark red, with a few pink varieties. There are, however, some fine distinctions in the way they grow, in the flower shapes and abundance of flowers, in the appearance of the leaves and in the degree of attractiveness of the flowerbuds, which gleam wine

"Scarlet Wonder". A vision of glowing colour and profuse flowers is provided by this Repens hybrid. It has attractive, curly petal edges (like "Bad Eilsen" and "Dr Ernst Schäle") and fresh green, crinkly, convex leaves with glowing red flowerbuds scattered among the foliage like tiny red lights.

red among deep green foliage in some varieties before the start of spring. Because of their cushion-like shape, Repens hybrids are ideal for planting in small gardens, courtyards or roof gardens. They can be placed in front of groups of small trees or taller shrubs, on semi-shady slopes or in flowerbeds. They also look good in large containers or planted in lieu of a low hedge, for example in a front garden. The varieties "Red Carpet" and "Scarlet Wonder" grow particularly low.

NB: As they flower very early, there is a danger of late frost damaging the flowers in regions with a less-temperate climate. Keep some form of frost protection handy, such as plastic bubble pack, conifer branches or polythene sheets, and cover the plants if there appears to be a risk of frost.

"Abendrot" is slightly sensitive to freezing temperatures but, in addition to beautiful flowers, it offers just about everything one could wish of a Repens hybrid: very prostrate growth, deep green foliage and decorative flowerbuds which are partially open very early indeed.

Wild varieties and their hybrids

Among these rhododendron species you will find some that have not been influenced by cultivating or have only been slightly changed by crossing. None the less, they are still very suitable for planting in gardens. Most of them have a cushion-like growth, producing up to 1 m (40 in) tall dwarf shrubs with brilliant blue, violet or white flowers. The flowering time of

Rhododendron russatum "Gletschernacht".

these different species ranges through the entire spring season right into the middle of summer. *R.* "Praecox" is a particularly early-flowering variety which opens delicate lilac-coloured flowers in gentle sunlight as early as the first month of spring.

Rhododendron ferrigineum "Tottenham". The 50-cm (20 in) tall dwarf shrub, with a width that is about double its height, has attractive dark green foliage which, come late spring/early summer, completely disappears under a flood of glorious pinky-violet flowers.

Rhododendrons from the group of wild species and their hybrids grow best in rockeries, flowerbeds or in a heathland garden. They are also suitable for planting in large containers and large tubs on balconies. They can be combined with other rhododendrons, wild herbaceous plants, small bulbs, heather or rockery plants or planted in front of flowering shrubs, bushes and trees, for example, Japanese cherry trees. Particularly low-growing varieties are: *R. impeditum* "Azurika", *R. carolinianum* "Dora Amateis", *R. camtschaticum* and *R. ferrugineum* "Tottenham".

NB: Wild rhododendrons will react extremely sensitively to too much fertilizing. I recommend not using fertilizer at all during the first year in which they are planted. Later, a third to half of the recommended amount for other rhododendrons will be quite sufficient.

Rhododendron camtschaticum is an enchanting dwarf rhododendron, only about 10-20 cm (4-8 in) tall, which, unfortunately, is not easy to cultivate. It requires a cool position and very high humidity. The long flowering period is a special feature: new flowers continue to appear from the first month of summer right through to the first month of autumn.

Rhododendron carolinianum "Dora Amateis" was created in the USA in 1955 and flowers at the beginning of the third month of spring. Because of its very slow growth – less than 35 cm (14 in) in ten years – it can be left in a large container for a long time.

Sun lovers

Deciduous azaleas

In contrast to the garden rhododendrons and Japanese azaleas,
these generally spreading, upright
azaleas (1.2-2 m/48-80 in) lose all
their leaves in winter. Several different types have been classified
according to their parent species or
their origins: the major group are
the Knap Hill hybrids, with large
flower umbels, blooming late
spring/early summer, the Mollis

An orange Genter azalea hybrid.

hybrids, with small, delicate growth
and an early flower, and the
Ponticum or Genter hybrids, which
are often scented.The range of
colours includes glowing shades of
orange, yellow and red, pink,
salmon pink and white. They look
best planted in front of conifers or
evergreen trees and shrubs.

"Coccinea Speciosa", a well-proven Genter hybrid with fiery orange flowers and a striking arrangement of branches in "storeys". It does not grow fast, so is very suitable for smaller gardens.

"Cécile" is one of the most popular standard varieties. It develops into an open, upright bush and produces enchanting 12-cm (4 in) wide umbels with huge, salmon pink, individual flowers which have a conspicuous golden yellow mark on the uppermost petal. The fresh green foliage presents a beautiful glowing-copper display when the new shoots form.

"Toucan" grows upright and spreading and sports elegant, creamy white flowers with large yellow markings, which start to open in the middle of the third month of spring. Unfortunately, this attractive variety is not often available.

"Goldtopas" has enchanting large, golden yellow flowers of unusual brilliance. They are made particularly impressive by an orange yellow mark on the inside of each flower. Its growth is spreading and very compact.

"Sylphides" lives up to its name with its delicate pink flowers. It has a faint scent and flowers as early as the beginning of the third month of spring. This cultivar was raised at the British tree nursery at Knap Hill.

"Homebush" is an extremely unusual variety. It is recognizable at a glance because of its spherical umbels which comprise semi-double, deep pink, star-shaped flowers. It blooms relatively late, towards the end of the first month of summer and its growth is open and upright.
NB: Deciduous azaleas need sunlight or they will rapidly stop flowering.

Japanese azaleas

These are also called evergreen azaleas as, in contrast to the deciduous azaleas, they retain all or part of their foliage in winter. As their name indicates, they come from Japan or are derived from Japanese ancestors. Gardening specialists distinguish several groups according to their cultivation and origins, but the amateur gardener need not worry about these classifications. Whereas the deciduous azaleas grow open and upright, Japanese azaleas develop into shrubs that spread out into almost cushion-like shapes that barely attain the height of 1 m (40 in). The flowers are arranged in small umbels, set very close together on the branches and almost completely covering the bush. The colour range includes shades similar to those of cyclamen flowers: purple violet, red, brilliant pink, delicate pink, salmon pink and brilliant white. They begin to flower early in the third month of spring and continue into the first month of summer. In autumn, the lower leaves, which later fall off, turn glorious shades of yellow, orange or red, while the young foliage on the shoot tips remains green. Japanese azaleas are particularly graceful flowering shrubs. They are ideal for planting by the edge of a pond, in a semi-shady rockery, along a stone-paved path or in courtyards. They can also be planted in a stone container or a large terracotta pot. The dwarf-sized Diamant azaleas are suitable for tubs.

"Blanice" has small but very profuse light pink flowers with red markings and matt to shiny, dark green leaves. It grows low and spreading and is much appreciated for its hardiness.

"Schneeglanz" has brilliant white, slightly fragrant flowers. Even quite young plants produce masses of flowers, which cover the light green foliage. It grows open and wide rather than prostrate.

In order to make it easier for you to choose from the wide range of Japanese azaleas, there follows a brief classification according to appearance:

Varieties with small flowers:
"Kermesina", "Kermesina Rosé", "Schneewittchen" – individual flowers that have a diameter of 3 cm (just over 1 in).

Large-flowered varieties:
"Blue Danube", "Georg Arends", "Geisha Orange", "Muttertag", "Rosalind" – individual flowers that have a diameter of 4.5-6 cm (1¾-2⅓ in).

Diamant azaleas: "Diamant Rot", "Diamant Rosa", "Diamant Weiss". A particularly small, prostrate-growing type with small flowers, obtainable in various colours.

NB: In winter, this type of azalea, which is rather sensitive to freezing temperatures, should always be covered with conifer branches.

"Geisha Orange". This large-flowered cultivar, created by Georg Arends from Wuppertal, Germany, first appeared on the market in the early 1970s. Its flowers are a particularly rare colour for a Japanese azalea. It blooms for a very long time and hardly loses any leaves in the winter.

Autumn colour
In autumn, many Japanese azaleas end the season with a display of glowing, wine red, orange or yellow foliage. Only the older leaves on the lower branches change colour. The tips of the shoots remain green all winter long.

"Rosalind". One of the most popular large-flowered varieties whose numerous pure pink flowers will not fade or discolour, even in a sunny position. It grows fairly open and sparse but spreading rather than high. It is considered to be hardy in temperatures above 24° C (75° F).

The rhododendron flowering calendar

	White	Yellow	Orange

	"Schneekrone"	*"Viscy"*	*"Coccinea Speciosa"*

Early to mid-spring	*R. dauricum var. album* (5)		
Mid-spring			
Mid-spring to late spring	"Gartendirektor Rieger" (3)	"Canary" (1) "Rothenburg" (3)	
Late spring	*R. carolinianum* "Dora Amateis" (5) "Cunningham's White" (1) "Koichiro Wada" (2) "Mont Blanc" (1) "Schneekrone" (2) "Schneespiegel" (1) "Silberwolke" (2) **Azaleas** "Toucan" (6)	"Ehrengold" (1) "Frühlingsgold" (2) "Goldbukett" (1) "Goldika" (1) "Goldkrone" (1) "Graf Lennart" (1) **Azaleas** *A. pontica* (6) "Nancy Waterer" (6) "Narzissiflora" (6)	"Abendsonne" (1) **Azaleas** "Geisha Orange" (7) "Orange Beauty" (7)
Late spring to early summer	"Gomer Waterer" (1) "Gudrun" (1) "Memoir" (1) "Schneebukett" (1) **Azaleas** "Davesii (6) "Diamant Weiss" (7) "Luzi" (7) "Möwe" (6) "Palestrina" (7) "Persil" (6) "Schneegold" (6) "Schneeglanz" (7) "Schneewittchen" (7)	"Babette" (2) "Flava" (2) "Lachsgold" (1) "Marietta" (2) "Marina" (1) "Viscy" (1) **Azaleas** "Golden Sunset" (6) "Goldpracht" (6) "Goldtopas" (6) "Klondyke" (6) "Sun Chariot" (6)	"Brasilia" (1) **Azaleas** "Coccinea Speciosa" (6) "Gibraltar" (6) "Golden Eagle" (6) Mollis x sinensis seedlings (6) "Polly Claessens" (6) "Rumba" (6) "Signalglühen" (7)
Early summer	"Album Novum" (1) "James Burchett" (1) "Silvia" (1)	"Inamorata" (1)	

1 = large-flowered hybrids; 2 = Yakushimanum hybrids; 3 = Williamsianum hybrids;

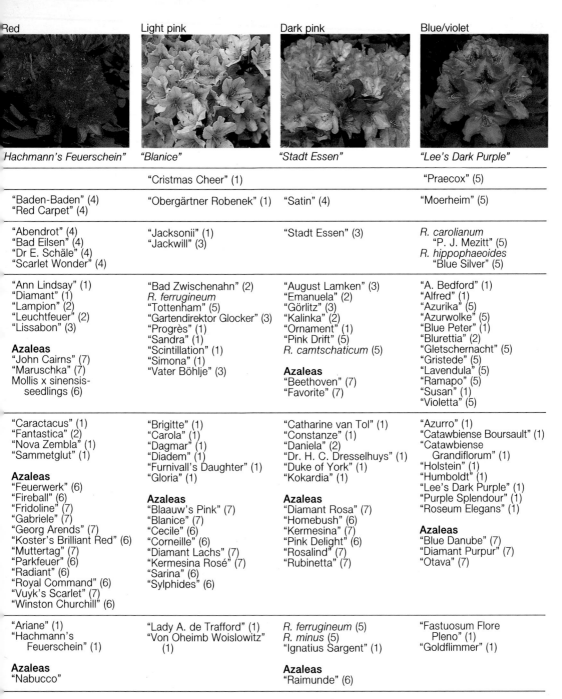

Red	Light pink	Dark pink	Blue/violet
"Hachmann's Feuerschein"	"Blanice"	"Stadt Essen"	"Lee's Dark Purple"
	"Cristmas Cheer" (1)		"Praecox" (5)
"Baden-Baden" (4) "Red Carpet" (4)	"Obergärtner Robenek" (1)	"Satin" (4)	"Moerheim" (5)

"Abendrot" (4)
"Bad Eilsen" (4)
"Dr E. Schäle" (4)
"Scarlet Wonder" (4)
	"Jacksonii" (1)
	"Jackwill" (3)
		"Stadt Essen" (3)	R. carolianum
			  "P. J. Mezitt" (5)
			R. hippophaeoides
			  "Blue Silver" (5)

"Ann Lindsay" (1) "Diamant" (1) "Lampion" (2) "Leuchtfeuer" (2) "Lissabon" (3) **Azaleas** "John Cairns" (7) "Maruschka" (7) Mollis x sinensis- seedlings (6)	"Bad Zwischenahn" (2) R. ferrugineum "Tottenham" (5) "Gartendirektor Glocker" (3) "Progrès" (1) "Sandra" (1) "Scintillation" (1) "Simona" (1) "Vater Böhlje" (3)	"August Lamken" (3) "Emanuela" (2) "Görlitz" (3) "Kalinka" (2) "Ornament" (1) "Pink Drift" (5) R. camtschaticum (5) **Azaleas** "Beethoven" (7) "Favorite" (7)	"A. Bedford" (1) "Alfred" (1) "Azurika" (5) "Azurwolke" (5) "Blue Peter" (1) "Blurettia" (2) "Gletschernacht" (5) "Gristede" (5) "Lavendula" (5) "Ramapo" (5) "Susan" (1) "Violetta" (5)
"Caractacus" (1) "Fantastica" (2) "Nova Zembla" (1) "Sammetglut" (1) **Azaleas** "Feuerwerk" (6) "Fireball" (6) "Fridoline" (7) "Gabriele" (7) "Georg Arends" (7) "Koster's Brilliant Red" (6) "Muttertag" (7) "Parkfeuer" (6) "Radiant" (6) "Royal Command" (6) "Vuyk's Scarlet" (7) "Winston Churchill" (6)	"Brigitte" (1) "Carola" (1) "Dagmar" (1) "Diadem" (1) "Furnivall's Daughter" (1) "Gloria" (1) **Azaleas** "Blaauw's Pink" (7) "Blanice" (7) "Cecile" (6) "Corneille" (6) "Diamant Lachs" (7) "Kermesina Rosé" (7) "Sarina" (6) "Sylphides" (6)	"Catharine van Tol" (1) "Constanze" (1) "Daniela" (2) "Dr. H. C. Dresselhuys" (1) "Duke of York" (1) "Kokardia" (1) **Azaleas** "Diamant Rosa" (7) "Homebush" (6) "Kermesina" (7) "Pink Delight" (6) "Rosalind" (7) "Rubinetta" (7)	"Azurro" (1) "Catawbiense Boursault" (1) "Catawbiense Grandiflorum" (1) "Holstein" (1) "Humboldt" (1) "Lee's Dark Purple" (1) "Purple Splendour" (1) "Roseum Elegans" (1) **Azaleas** "Blue Danube" (7) "Diamant Purpur" (7) "Otava" (7)

"Ariane" (1)
"Hachmann's
  Feuerschein" (1)
 	
Azaleas
"Nabucco"
	"Lady A. de Trafford" (1)
	"Von Oheimb Woislowitz"
	  (1)
		R. ferrugineum (5)
		R. minus (5)
		"Ignatius Sargent" (1)
		
		Azaleas
		"Raimunde" (6)
			"Fastuosum Flore
			  Pleno" (1)
			"Goldflimmer" (1)

4 = Repens hybrids; 5 = wild species or related hybrids; 6 = deciduous azaleas; 7 = Japanese azaleas

A Japanese garden

The characteristic elegance and tranquillity of traditional Japanese gardens hold a particular fascination for Westerners. With the help of rhododendrons and, in particluar, the evergreen azalea varieties, anyone can create a Japanese atmosphere. Some of the best sites in which to do this are by the edge of a pond or pool where the brilliant cascades of flowers will be mirrored in the still surface of the water, or in combination with a tranquil, uniformly green expanse of lawn.

Of course, the neighbouring plants should also provide a flavour of the Far East. The Japanese cherry tree, *Primula japonica*, fir trees, Japanese guelder rose (*Viburnum plicatum*), *Carex plantaginea* and Japanese forest grass are all eminently suitable for this purpose. The final touch could be provided by an ornamental stone lantern. Alternatively, even two or three large, beautifully shaped, natural stones can be very attractive.

A hint of Japan
This garden is an example of the successful blending of European and Japanese garden design in a setting of tranquil green lawns and tall conifers.

Rhododendron care all year round

Choosing the right position will be a key factor if you are to grow rhododendrons successfully. Further steps to success are the right choice of plants and correct planting. In addition, proper attention and correct feeding are vital for the well-being of your shrubs.

Buying and transporting your plants

It is important to find out when and where you can obtain healthy, vigorous shrubs. You must also be aware of the signs of good quality and know how to identify a plant that is free from disease.

The best time to buy and plant
The best time for planting is from the first month of spring through to the middle of the last month of spring, or from the beginning of autumn until the middle of the first month of winter. This will give the shrubs enough time to root well before the beginning of the summer months when there is less rainfall, or until the first frosts, respectively. *Exceptions:* Theoretically, container plants can be planted all year round but the best chance of success will be achieved if you keep to spring or autumn planting.

Where to buy rhododendrons
There are several ways of buying your shrubs. The right one for you will depend on your requirements and on whether you are able to transport your own plants.
Tree nurseries will offer a select, basic range of high quality and can often provide various sizes of the same varieties.
Garden centres generally sell shrubs of good quality but the range of plants to choose from will very much depend on the size of the outlet.
Specialist tree nurseries and rhododendron growers are ideal if you are looking for rarer varieties or very new cultivars. In either case, you should be able to obtain high grade, quality plants at very reasonable prices.
Some supermarkets or hypermarkets sell plants. These are not subject to any kind of quality control but are very inexpensive.
Mail order firms often have lower prices than tree nurseries.

However, the selection is often rather limited and the plants are generally sold by description, for example, "large-flowered, red", and are not identified by a species or variety name. The advantage is that they are delivered to your doorstep.

My tip: Make sure to order your plants in plenty of time as the rarer varieties, in particular, will go out of stock rather quickly. The catalogues produced by specialist tree nurseries, some of which include a wealth of colour photos, offer an excellent guide through the maze of available rhododendrons. The small fee charged for the catalogue is usually refunded or deducted, even on small orders.

How are rhododendrons sold?
About 90% of all rhododendrons arrive on the market with a proper rootstock; the remainder are sold as large container plants, which means that they are in pots. Plants with rootstocks grow rapidly and their prices are a great deal more favourable than those of container plants. The latter have the advantage, however, of being plantable all year round as they do not depend on frost-free periods.

Size and quality
The sizes of plants on the market usually depend on the rhododendron group to which each plant belongs. Large-flowered hybrids, for example, are nearly always sold when they have reached heights of 30-40 cm (12-16 in), 40-50 cm (16-20 in) and 50-60 cm (20-24 in).

The azalea (Rhododendron simsii) will flower indoors during the winter.

As a rule, Japanese azaleas are sold when they have grown to a height of 25-30 cm (10-12 in).

The signs of good quality are:
● a firm rootstock that corresponds to the size of the plant, with a diameter of about half the size of the crown of foliage;
● low, regular growth with lots of branches, even at the lower levels of the plant;
● dark green, healthy foliage;
● a profusion of buds.

Grafted rhododendrons

These are rhododendrons which have been grafted on to the rootstock of a more robust species or variety. Grafted rhododendrons possess a number of advantages. They are healthier, grow better and produce more flowers, react less sensitively to chalky soil and can tolerate a lack of water better than non-grafted ones. They are, however, slightly more expensive because raising them is more time-consuming but, over the years, this additional cost will more than justify itself.

Unfortunately, it is not always easy to tell if a plant has been grafted, even for the expert. If you are dealing with a reputable tree nursery, however, you can be sure that you really will receive grafted plants.

Planting

Transporting your plants

Garden centres and tree nurseries with high standards of customer service will generally pack the plants in such a way that you only need to stand or lie the plants in the boot of your car.

Preparing rhododendrons for transport:
● The rootstock should be protected by a plastic bag so that it cannot dry out and your car will be kept clean.
● If larger plants are involved, tie up the branches so that they cannot break off.
● If your plants have to be transported on a roof rack, even if it is only over a short distance, they should be wrapped in polythene (peat sacks or dustbin liners are ideal).
● Make sure the label bearing the picture and variety name of your plant is not lost in transport.

When you reach home: If possible, remove your plants from the car immediately and unpack them. Stand the shrubs in water for ten minutes, even if the rootstock still seems moist. If you cannot plant them right away, stand the plants in a cool, shady place, for example, in a garage. If longer waiting periods are foreseen, heel in the plants

provisionally in a shady spot in the garden, which is the equivalent to planting them loosely.

When plants arrive by mail order

Remember that the plants may have been in the post for several days. For this reason, you must open the package immediately it arrives and remove the packaging material. Stand the plants in water for ten minutes and, if possible, plant them the same day or prepare them for planting (see above).

My tip: Very dry rootstocks will absorb water more easily if you squirt a little washing-up liquid into it.

Planting and caring for rhododendrons in the garden

NB: Before planting your newly purchased plants in the garden, you should have prepared the optimal conditions for them (see p. 10). Do not plant them until these requirements have been met.

Planting correctly
● Dig a hole that is about twice as deep and three times as wide as the size of the rootstock.
● Mix the excavated soil with moist peat or special rhododendron potting soil in a ratio of 1:1.
● Fill up the hole with half of this mixture and set the rhododendron in it.
● If you are planting rhododendrons in containers, gently scratch the surface of the rootstock all round with a handrake. If the rootstock has come equipped with a covering, untie this and fold it down all round.
● Finally, fill the hole all round with soil and press it down gently with your foot.

Dig a hole and mix the extracted soil with peat in a ratio of 1:1. Place the rhododendron (still tied up) in the hole. Fill the hole with soil and press it down gently with your foot. Do not cut the string until this point. Larger plants will need some support. Drive a stake diagonally past the rootstock into the ground.

If the soil is heavy, do not press it down as this will make it too hard! The shrub should be placed in the ground at such a depth that the rootstock is barely covered with soil. Rhododendrons that are planted too deep will not grow well and their leaves will turn yellow.

● Make a watering trench around the plant by heaping up an earth wall about 10 cm (4 in) high all around it. This will prevent water from running away too fast and help to direct it towards the roots.
● Give the plants plenty of water to begin with.
● Larger shrubs (over 1.5 m or 60 in tall) need a strong wooden support stick to prevent them from being uprooted by strong winds. Drive the stake diagonally past the rootstock into the ground and then tie the rhododendron to it with hemp, not nylon, rope.

A whole bed of rhododendrons

If you are intending to plant a whole bed with rhododendrons, the best method of getting an idea as to how the final picture will look is first just to stand all the plants in their approximate positions. In this way you can still shift the shrubs around until you think you have got it right. Mark the chosen spots before starting to plant.

General rule for spacing the plants:
The right distance between the plants is twice the height of one shrub. Example: 50-cm (20 in) high plants should be planted at a distance of 1 m (40 in) (measured from one stem to the other), 1.5-m (59 in) high shrubs at a distance of 3 m (118 in) and so on.
NB: If the rhododendrons do grow too large they can easily be transplanted.

Care after planting

A rhododendron will take about eight weeks to root properly and during that time it will need a lot of attention. Later on, it will manage with relatively little care.

Four steps to success
1. Make sure the soil is sufficiently moist. Once soil containing peat has completely dried out, it will not absorb water very readily.
2. Increase the humidity of the surrounding air during a dry period (see p. 15).
3. During a spell of persistently sunny weather (particularly if this is combined with severe frosts), make sure there is some shade (see p. 45).
4. If you have planted your rhododendrons in the spring, do not fertilize them for the first time until at least three weeks after planting and, at the very latest, shortly after the flowering period. If the rhododendrons were planted in the autumn, do not fertilize them until the following mid-spring (see fertilizing programme, p. 42).

(see p. 15). ... (see p. 45). ... (see fertilizing programme, p. 42).

Regular care – the basic essentials

These measures of basic care are important if you want your rhododendrons to thrive for many years:
● correct watering
● proper fertilizing (see p. 42)
● mulching (see p. 44)
● further care (see p. 44)
● protection in winter (see p. 45)
● transplanting (see p. 45)

(see p. 42) ... (see p. 44) ... (see p. 44) ... (see p. 45) ... (see p. 45)

Correct watering

Once they have rooted properly, rhododendrons can cope astonishingly well with occasional periods of drought (up to two to three weeks without rain). If you are dealing with extremely long periods of drought and high temperatures simultaneously, artificial irrigation may become necessary, particularly during the flowering period and when new shoots are growing and the need for water is correspondingly greater. Periods with very little rain are quite useful during the summer months when too much moisture would cause the plants to shoot again, which is not a good thing shortly before the onset of winter.

The rules of watering
1. It is time to water whenever the soil seems dry up to 3 cm (1 in) below the surface of the ground.
2. The best devices for watering are garden sprinklers and hoses with spray attachments. A watering time of two to three hours is necessary to moisten the soil sufficiently.
3. If you are using a hose, depending on the size of the plant, lay the nozzle close to the stem for five to twenty minutes and allow the water to seep in slowly. After that, depending on the type of soil you have, you may not need to water again for eight to ten days.
4. During fine weather, water either in the evening or early in the morning, so that the foliage can dry before the sunlight becomes intense. If possible, do not water around midday. When sunbeams hit waterdrops at an acute angle, they work like tiny magnifying glasses and can cause burn damage to the foliage.
5. If the plants are drying out, water them immediately. Typical symptoms are limp leaves and shoot tips and leaves that are curling up.

Fertilizing programme

Rhododendron group	Early to mid-spring	Late spring/early summer*
Rhododendron-hybrids and deciduous azaleas (small plants – up to 60 cm or 24 in)	50 g (1½ oz) horn chips and 50 g mineral compound fertilizer or controlled-release fertilizer	50 g (1¾ oz) mineral compound fertilizer
(large plants)	100 g (3½ oz) horn chips and 100 g mineral compound fertilizer or controlled-release fertilizer	70 g (2½ oz) mineral compound fertilizer
Wild species and dwarf varieties	25 g (¾ oz) horn chips and 10 g (⅓ oz) mineral compound fertilizer or controlled-release fertilizer	
Japanese azaleas	50 g (1¾ oz) horn chips and 50 g mineral compound fertilizer or controlled-release fertilizer	*Disregard if controlled-release fertilizer was used for fertilizing in spring.

If this happens and the plants are not watered for another few days, the leaves will dry up and drop off. Young shoots are most vulnerable.
Watering before the winter: If the soil has become very dry during the autumn, which seldom happens, all evergreen rhododendrons and azaleas must be watered once more, very thoroughly, so that they have a sufficient store of moisture before the temperature drops below freezing. During the winter, they will need watering only occasionally, during periods of very dry weather, but never while the ground is frozen.

The right water
Rhododendrons require soft water. Hard water is full of lime or chalk and is not good for them. Ask your local water authority about the degree of hardness in your mains water. If your water is hard, which means the value is over 13 degrees Clark (ask your water authority), if possible, use rainwater instead. If you are unable to water your plants with rainwater, as a last resort, you may be able to soften your mains water by using sulphuric acid or oxalic acid: 1 cm of concentrated sulphuric acid or 2.5 g oxalic acid to 100 litres (22 gal) water will reduce the degree of hardness by a factor of 1.

My tip: A much better method is to make sure the soil retains moisture so that frequent watering will not be necessary; this can be accomplished with a thin, annually renewed layer of mulch.

Fertilizing
Sufficient fertilizing is very important for the health of your rhododendron plants because their abundant foliage means that they require large quantities of nutrients. Fertilizing increases the plants' ability to grow healthy-looking foliage and aids the development of plenty of buds.
Keep to the fertilizing periods stipulated (see fertilizing programme, above). Do not fertilize any more after the middle of summer!
General rule for nutrient requirements: The leaves of a rhododendron are a good indicator: the larger they are, the more fertilizing they will need. Large-flowered hybrids, with their large, strong leaves, will need a great deal more fertilizer than the small-leaved Japanese azaleas.
Symptoms of nutrient deficiency: Leaves that are light green all over, an increase in falling leaves, sparse development of buds and flowers, sparse growth and few new shoots (see p. 48). You can obtain the right kinds of fertilizer through the gardening trade. There are several different types, which vary in their composition and effect.

My tip: Do not confuse special rhododendron soils with fertilizers. This special soil, which is mainly composed of peat, has merely been enriched with fertilizer. It is not an adequate substitute for a compound fertilizer.

A symphony in red and pink
A harmonious blend is particularly important when using the brilliant colours of rhododendrons and azaleas.

Mineral fertilizers

These are fast-working, have an immediate effect and are usually sold in the form of granules. Sprinkle them on the surface of the soil, in a circle round the shrub, with a diameter that corresponds to the spreading foliage of the shrub and about 20 cm (8 in) away from the stem. Then rake them in.

● Mineral compound fertilizer contains all three of the essential main nutrients: nitrogen (chemical symbol N), phosphorous (P) and potassium (K). Also included are the essential trace elements in a balanced ratio. I have had good results with commercial preparations bought from garden centres. There are plenty of well-known brands to choose from.

● Mineral, controlled-release, compound fertilizers have become much more popular over recent years. These long-term fertilizers are manufactured in such a way that they will release the nutrients (in particular, water-soluble nitrogen) into the soil very gradually. The advantage of this is that the fertilizing effect should last for up to six months, which means you will only need to fertilize once, in the spring. In addition, controlled-release fertilizer is environmentally friendly as it does not allow nitrogen to be washed into the deeper levels of the soil. There are various well-known brands on the market and you can find out more about these at your local garden centre.

Organic fertilizers

These may be plant- or animal-based and will release nutrients quite slowly (particularly nitrogen). This means that their effect is long-term and therefore they should only be used for a main fertilizing in the spring. I have used both horn chips and horn meal successfully. Another useful organic fertilizer is well-decomposed stable manure, which can be distributed under your plants in a layer 1-3 cm (up to 1 in) thick, depending on the size of the plant.

Iron- and magnesium-rich fertilizer

This is a remedy for acute iron or magnesium deficiency (see chlorosis, p. 49) caused by a pH factor that is too high. Their effect will last for only a few months, then the procedure will have to be repeated. Check with your garden centre etc. for commercially available products.

Mulching

Rhododendrons only feel comfortable in loose, humus-rich soil. This type of soil is formed in places where soil micro-organisms are very active. Mulching will increase this activity; the layer of mulching distributed over the surface represents "food" and will incite the micro-organisms to greater levels of activity. Various types of organic matter can be employed for mulching: peat, semi-decomposed leaf mould, fine wood shavings and grass clippings are all useful. Mulching should be carried out once a year, preferably in autumn. The mulching layer should be 3 cm (1 in) thick and should be spread on the soil in a circle corresponding to the spread of the crown of foliage.

Advantages of mulching: I can readily recommend this method of care to every rhododendron enthusiast, as mulching produces new humus. Additionally, the soil will remain loose and porous, will stay moist longer and weeds will be suffocated at an early stage.

Further care

Apart from regular fertilizing, rhododendrons really do not need a great deal of care. The most important measures are as follows:

Removing dead flowers

Removing withered flowerheads is particularly recommended for young plants that have attained a height of 1 m (40 in). This prevents essential nutrients, which the shrub needs for growth, being wasted on the unnecessary formation of seeds. Deadheading also allows the young shoots, which form at the base of the flower stalks, more room to develop. The best time to deadhead flowers is immediately after flowering. Do this gently so that any young shoots that have begun to develop are not damaged or broken off along with the faded flowers.

Deadheading

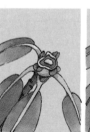

Do this immediately after the flower has faded, as soon as the petals have withered. Be careful not to damage the buds of shoots situated below the flowers while removing them! Removing the flowerheads gives the young shoots enough room to unfold.

Removing new shoots

Removing new shoots, or pinching out as it is usuallly called, will encourage open, sparsely growing rhododendron shrubs to develop denser, more compact growth. Simply pinch out any new shoots as they appear. This will activate the leaf buds along the sides of the branch and three or more young shoots per branch will develop instead.

Pruning

Generally speaking, rhododendrons should not be pruned. There are, however, some exceptions. Pruning will be necessary if:
● the plants have become too big for the position in which they are growing and they cannot be transplanted because of lack of space;
● they are too old, lanky or are beginning to become bare from the bottom up;
● individual branches have broken off due to the weight of snow, strong winds or for other reasons. The most favourable time for cutting back is from early to mid-spring.

My tip: If a lot of pruning is necessary, for example, in order to completely reshape a shrub, do not do all the cutting at once but cut back only half of the shrub one year and the rest the following year.

How to prune

Use sharp clippers to cut off individual branches just above a leaf axil. In just a few weeks' time new leaves will develop from the buds on the remaining branches.
Some varieties respond particularly well to pruning. These include "Catawbiense Boursault", "Catawbiense Grandiflorum", "Cunningham's White", "English Roseum" and "Roseum Elegans". For this reason, gardeners often like to use these varieties as hedges.

Pruning

Rhododendrons that are rather old and are becoming bare from below, can be rejuvenated by cutting them back in the spring. Always cut above a leaf axil. In early summer, the bare branches will start producing new leaves.

Winter protection

Most rhododendrons that are for sale in tree nurseries etc. should be sufficiently hardy for your local climate. Occasionally, however, in unfavourable conditions, some frost damage may occur. The main enemy – as for all evergreen plants – is bright winter sunlight coupled with severe frosts. In such conditions, the sun thaws out the leaves and then moisture evaporates from them but cannot be replenished from the frozen soil via the root system. In actual fact, most frost damage is really damage caused by drying out.
Some species, like the sensitive Japanese azaleas, respond to the threat of drying out by shedding part of their foliage; the large-flowered hybrids curl up their leaves.
Shading: You can help your plants to overwinter successfully by setting up reed mats or canvas screens to provide shade. In the case of small shrubs, it will be sufficient to push a few conifer branches into the soil around the shrubs.

Transplanting

If a plantation of rhododendrons becomes too dense over the years, they can still be transplanted quite easily, even at a great age, because of their shallow, flat-rooting systems. The best time for this is mid-spring or early autumn.

How to transplant:

● Tie the plant up in such a way that no branches will accidentally break off during the move. You will also be able to get at the rootstock more easily.
● Use a spade to cut carefully all the way round the rootstock to about two spade-depths down, and at a distance from the stem that corresponds to about two-thirds of the diameter of the crown of foliage.
● Replant the shrub in a new position (planting, see p. 40).

Rhododendrons as large container plants

Rhododendron enthusiasts who have no garden need not abandon their ambition to grow their own plants. Many of these colourful shrubs can be grown in pots, large containers or tubs (suitable varieties, see p. 47).

Choosing the right container
Rhododendrons and azaleas are flat-rooting plants and will require broad, shallow containers rather than deep ones. Depending on their rate of growth, 30-40-cm (12-16 in) deep containers, with a diameter of 60-100 cm (24-40 in), may be sufficient. Japanese azaleas and dwarf rhododendrons will even flourish in large balcony boxes.
NB: The plant container must have sufficiently large drainage holes in the base and should be made out of a porous material, like wood or clay, as the fine roots will react sensitively to lack of oxygen and waterlogging.

Soil
Rhododendrons require humus-rich, acid soil of a loose consistency in their pots or containers, just as they would in the garden. The ideal soil can be mixed out of commercially produced rhododendron soil (ask at your garden centre etc.) with coarse sand in a ratio of 5:1, or you can make up your own soil using leaf mould or lime-free composting soil, peat and coarse sand in a ratio of 2:2:1. No matter which soil mixture you decide on, it should always have some basic fertilizer mixed in with it. A mineral controlled-release fertilizer is very suitable (ask at your garden centre etc. for a good brand) as it will gradually release the nutrients over a period of six months.

Drainage
Good drainage is essential so you must make sure some form of drainage is present to help surplus water to run away. Fill the bottom of the plant container with a 5-cm (2 in) layer of coarse gravel or sand and cover it with a piece of interfacing material so that the drainage layer does not become clogged up with soil. Then fill the pot up with soil.

My tip: You can obtain drainage sheets made of polystyrene through the building trade. These are very practical and extremely light in weight, which is a plus when you consider the total weight of the plant container.

Planting time
Early spring and early autumn are equally suitable times. Planting in spring has the advantage that you will not have to wait so long before enjoying the flowers. My experience, however, is that shrubs planted in the autumn seem to root faster and better.

The right position
Rhododendrons in large containers do not differ from their relatives in gardens. They all need semi-shady positions or a spot that is in shade part of the time. All positions should be sheltered from the wind.
Very suitable: west-facing balconies and patios or sheltered, east-facing positions (if necessary provide protection in winter, see p. 45).
Not suitable: hot, very sunny, south-facing balconies or patios, north-facing positions that are always in the shade or windy or draughty positions.

Care during the summer
Watering: Make the sure the soil is always moist, as rhododendrons that have to cope with constant dryness are very susceptible to diseases and pests.
On warm, dry days, water daily, preferably with water that has been standing outside, rainwater or softened mains water (see p. 42).
In changeable weather, or if the weather is not very warm, water when necessary but do not wait until the leaves are hanging down limply, which would indicate a dire need of water.
Fertilizing: As plants in large containers have to cope with a limited area for their rooting systems, regular fertilizing will be necessary. Having said that, fertilizing is a very simple business and generally means one dose of controlled-release fertilizer. A handful (about 50 g or 1 oz) sprinkled on the soil in mid- to late spring will be sufficient. During the summer the nutrients will be released gradually and washed into the soil every time you water the plants. Japanese azaleas and dwarf rhododendrons should receive only a third of this recommended dose.
Further care: Withered flowers must be removed (see deadheading, p. 44) as the formation of seeds uses up the plants' energy. Pinch out shoots right from the start to make the shrub grow bushy and compact, unless, of course, it is a particularly compact variety anyway (pinching out, see p. 45).

Winter care
Rhododendrons in large containers can be left standing on a balcony or patio during the winter. Observe the same procedures as for plants in the garden (see p. 45), which mainly means ensuring that the plants are not subjected to strong sunlight, particularly in the mornings and around midday.
Watering in winter requires a little bit of thought.
Check the soil of plants in large

Japanese azaleas in pots are suitable for patios and roof gardens. Shown here is the variety "Favorite".

containers in positions that are sheltered from the rain to see if the soil is still moist. Too much water can be a problem, particularly if proper drainage has not been provided. If you press the soil in a large container with your finger and it "squeaks" with wetness, you must cover the plant and container with a polythene sheet or a peat sack before the next snow or rain shower.

Suitable varieties for large containers

All small and compact-growing rhododendron and azalea varieties, as well as Repens hybrids, Williamsianum hybrids, Yakushimanum hybrids, most wild species and their hybrids and Japanese azaleas. You can even have large-flowered hybrids, as long as you choose compact, low-growing varieties. Suitable large-flowered hybrids are "Gudrun", "Schneespiegel", "Mont Blanc"

(white); "Goldika", "Goldkrone", "Graf Lennart" (yellow); "Ariane", "Hachmann's Feuerschein" (red); "Progrès", "Dagmar", "Brigitte", "Gloria", "Ornament" (pink); "Blue Peter" and "Azzuro" (violet). Among the deciduous azaleas the varieties "Goldtopas" and "Coccinea Speciosa" are particularly suitable for large containers.

If you have only a large balcony box for planting, the Diamant azaleas from the group of Japanese azaleas will flourish extremely well.

Diseases and pests

Like most plants, rhododendrons are naturally equipped with good health and are resistant to most diseases and pests. As a rule, they will only become vulnerable to infestation with bacteria, harmful insects and fungal diseases if they are incorrectly cared for or grown in an unsuitable position.

Symptoms of weakness and disease

It is the leaves that will show the first signs of any problems the plant may be experiencing. They will display discoloration, malformation and signs of being eaten. More rarely, branches and buds may also display symptoms of disease.

Physiological damage

This term is used to describe diseases that are caused by a nutrient deficiency or by an excess of water, light, hot or cold temperature or nutrients. The debilitated state of the plant will then make it particularly susceptible to attack by fungi, bacteria and harmful insects.

Light green or yellow foliage has many causes:

● Lack of nitrogen. This is recognizable by light green or yellow green discoloration of the leaves and also by a particularly noticeable loss of leaves during the entire summer. Remedy: short-term treatment with rapidly effective liquid fertilizer (ask at your garden centre etc.) or, in the long term, with balanced fertilizing (fertilizing, see p. 42).

NB: If the loss of leaves is not too severe, there is no need to worry. All evergreen plants lose some of their leaves at regular intervals.

● Chlorosis: yellow discoloration usually starts between the veins of the leaves although the leaves themselves are still green to begin with. Light yellow shoots in spring; in severe cases they may even be white. Cause and remedy, see table, page 49.

● Waterlogging or dense soil: will cause similar symptoms to lack of nitrogen and chlorosis and, in addition, will cause noticeably lacklustre foliage. Remedy: dig up the plants in the spring or autumn, loosen the soil, provide a drainage layer (gravel, sand or broken pieces of pot) at the bottom of the hole, and then replant the shrubs.

● Sun burn: symptoms are light yellow leaves, often with irregular, brownish burn marks on the "sunny side" of the plant. Cause: a position that is too sunny, lacking in humidity. Remedy: shading (see p. 45) but, better still, plant the shrub in a more favourable position.

Weak growth, lazy to flower: caused by general lack of nutrients. Remedy: proper fertilizing.

Limp or curled up leaves: This is the plant's natural protection against evaporation during freezing temperatures or because of lack of water. Remedy: during the summer, water immediately and provide shade. In winter, do nothing. As soon as the frosts cease, the leaves will recover by themselves.

Cracks in the bark, on the stems and branches: These are caused by late, severe frosts in the spring when the sap has already begun to rise again. Remedy: immediately tie raffia tightly around the affected places so that the bark and the wood are held together.

Dry spots along leaf edges and along the central veins of leaves: damage due to frost or dryness. Remedy: in future, protect your plants better against winter sunlight and water them regularly.

Brown edges of leaves and leaf tips: these may indicate a high concentration of salt in the soil, caused by over-fertilizing. Remedy: see "over-fertilizing" in the table on page 49.

Fungal diseases

The cause of fungal infestation is nearly always a general weakness of the plant. Usually, it is the leaves that are affected, more rarely the buds. Some types of fungi manage to penetrate right into the wood and may endanger the life of the rhododendron. You will find a description of the symptoms and methods of control for fungi that commonly attack rhododendrons in the table on page 50.

Pests

Included among pests are harmful insects, spider mites and other mites. They will eat the leaves or suck the sap and often cause considerable damage. In addition, they will, of course, adversely affect the appearance of the plant. The most common types are described in the table on the right.

Plant protection agents

There is a confusing number of plant protection agents on the market. Usually the ingredients will be listed on the packaging but, generally, these names will mean nothing to anyone but an expert. When seeking a protection agent against a specific disease or pest, the best course of action is to seek specialist advice at your local garden centre. Where possible, always try to use environmentally friendly, biological forms of control.

Warning: Always make sure that you keep any such preparations out of the reach of children or pets and that you follow the manufacturer's instructions exactly.

Chemical plant protection agents

Three different types can be distinguished:
● insecticides = substances to control insects;
● fungicides = substances to control fungal diseases;
● acaricides = substances for the control of spider mites.

How plant protection agents work:

Some substances work externally on diseases and pests and are sprinkled, poured or sprayed on.

By contrast, other substances are used to penetrate the plant via leaves or roots and thus reach all parts of the plant. These are called systemic substances.

Mistakes in care and infestation by pests

Chlorosis: This is usually caused by soil with a pH factor over 7. This means iron and magnesium, which the plant needs for the development of chlorophyll, cannot be absorbed by the plant. Remedy: short-term treatment with fertilizer containing iron and magnesium; long-term, lower the pH factor.

Over-fertilizing: dry, brown edges and tips of the leaves all over the plant, caused by too much or too concentrated a dosage of liquid or mineral fertilizers. Remedy: immediately water the root area thoroughly so that the fertilizer is washed away.

Scale insects: the leaves appear dull green with varnish-like excretions on their undersides. This usually appears in late spring/early summer in positions with too little humidity and too much sunlight. Remedy: change the position or improve the existing one. In severe cases, treat with an insecticide.

Red spider mite, white mites, rhododendron bug: dull green leaves and malformed shoot tips. Infestation usually occurs in positions that are too dry. Remedy: short-term treatment with an acaricide; long-term, improve or change the position of the shrubs.

Vine weevils: a tiny beetle which is active at night and eats crescent-shaped holes out of the edges of the leaves. Its whitish larvae live in the soil and may damage the roots and neck of the roots, so that the plant dies. Remedy: in less severe cases, pick off all the beetles.

If infestation with vine weevils is severe, destroy the larvae around the roots and base of the stem. In early autumn and mid-spring respectively, water the plants twice thoroughly at an interval of two weeks with a 0.1 % solution of commercial insecticide. If large container plants are infested, try nematodes (alternative plant protection, see p. 50).

● The advantage of systemic substances is that even pests lurking under leaves are caught so that one application may be sufficient.

● The disadvantage of systemic substances is that they will travel through the sap into the flowers and may endanger useful insects there. For this reason, systemic substances should not be employed while buds are opening nor throughout the entire flowering period.

Biological plant protection agents

In recent years, attempts have been made to find and use environmentally friendly, biological methods to protect all kinds of plants. Good results have been obtained with the use of nematodes (tiny thread-like worms which act as parasites on insects). They attack the larvae of vine weevils and are particularly recommended for plants in pots and large containers. To find a good source for these, enquire at your garden centre or local plant nursery.

Alternative plant protection

This term is used to describe home remedies. Among these are herb teas and brews, which are used to strengthen the plants' defences so they will not become infested with diseases and pests in the first place. Other possibilities are employing plants whose odour gets rid of pests, removing pests by hand or cutting off parts of plants infested with fungi.

Prevention against fungal diseases

One excellent remedy is mare's tail brew (*Hippuris vulgaris*): leave 500 g (1 lb) of fresh or 100 g (3½ oz) dried mare's tail to soak in 5 litres (9 pt) of water for 24 hours, then boil it for 45 minutes and strain it after cooling. Dilute the brew with water

Fungal diseases

Spotted leaf disease: reddish-brown spots with darker rims starting at the leaf tips and edges, caused by *Phyllosticta*. Remedy: break off affected leaves and burn them, improve the position of the shrub and, in severe cases, treat the shrub with a fungicide (take a leaf sample to your garden centre and ask for advice).

Spotted leaf disease: irregular, dark, reddish-edged spots, caused by *Cercospora rhododendri*. Remedy: as above, mainly by improving the position of the plant (see position, p. 10). Plant protection agents will only provide temporary relief.

Sooty mould (*Apio sporium*): a sticky substance on the leaves caused by a fungus which lives on the excretions of aphids. Common on plants situated under densely foliated trees. Remedy: provide more light among the trees by cutting them back so that more air and rainwater can reach the shrubs.

Dying branches or silver leaf: the leaves of entire branches may suddenly dry out. Caused by a fungus, *Phytophtora*, which may penetrate via tiny wounds. Remedy: rigorously cut back affected branches and burn them; spray with fungicide (check with your garden centre etc).

Brown buds: caused by the rhododendron leafhopper. Remedy: pinch out affected buds before the end of spring and burn them. In severe cases – when you touch the plant, dozens of leafhoppers jump out – spray with insecticide in late summer.

My tip: When preparing the mare's tail brew for spraying, mix in three drops of washing-up liquid to stop the water from forming "beads" on the leaf surface and dripping off. This will help to distribute the liquid more evenly and to keep it on the plant.

in the proportions 1:5 and spray the plant with this it at fortnightly intervals.

To combat vine weevils, lay a few old, damp planks in the area below the leaves of the infested shrub. The weevils will be encouraged to use these as a hiding place. Each morning, check them and collect the weevils.

Further possibilities of alternative plant protection may be found in gardening magazines and modern gardening handbooks.

Pest control using local wildlife

Many pests will be unable to multiply so easily in a garden if their natural enemies are provided with particularly good conditions. Among the natural predators of harmful insects are, for example, birds, hedgehogs, small weasels, shrews, bats, frogs and toads, snakes, slow worms and lizards, but many insects are also useful, such as ladybirds, lacewing flies, ichneumon flies and hover flies. Try to do something towards providing all these useful helpers with suitable hiding places so that they will feel at home in your garden and do their bit towards pest control. Natural hedges and nest boxes will provide ideal nesting places for birds and a pond will encourage frogs and toads. Leave a corner of your garden untouched for wild plants and do not thin out shrubs too rigorously, and you may soon find that a hedgehog has moved in. Once some of these creatures have made a home in your garden, you will find there are far fewer pests.

Handling and using plant protection agents

Chemical and many biological or alternative plant protection agents may not only be dangerous for pests, they may also endanger or harm other animals – and humans. For this reason you must take great care when you use these preparations and observe the following basic points:

● Always follow the advice on the packaging meticulously. If you are not sure about a detail, ask the expert from whom you bought the preparation.

● Dilute the preparation exactly as described in the instructions. Too high a concentration may harm the plant and too weak a solution may not have the desired result.

● Listen to the weather report beforehand. If rain is on the way, no amount of misting or spraying will have an effect as the substance will be washed off. Avoid spraying anything on windy days too. You might inhale the plant protection agent or some of it might drift into other parts of the garden where it could cause damage, for example, among your vegetables or in a fishpond.

● Use the finest setting of the nozzle when spraying, so that as little of the liquid as possible drips on to the ground. This will protect both the soil and the ground water.

● Do not use chemical plant protection agents at the first glimpse of pests. On the other hand, do not wait until the entire plant is completely infested, as this may mean having to use a larger amount of chemical than you would if you had started trying to control the problem earlier on. Used at the correct time, one application should be sufficient.

● Make sure that neither children nor pets come into contact with plant protection agents.

Aerosol gases

For the sake of the environment, avoid using any kind of spray cans or sprays containing aerosols. Use pump-action spray cans which are obtainable in various sizes in the garden trade. If you have a large rhododendron plantation, use a piston pump or a compression pump to spray your shrubs.

My tip: If you do not wish to purchase one of these rather expensive larger spraying devices, ask your garden centre or somewhere similar if they hire out such equipment.

Finding out more

Advice on all aspects of plant protection can be obtained from garden centres, nurseries, the relevant departments of agricultural colleges, etc. Usually, this advice is free. A fee will only be incurred if a great deal of time-consuming research is needed. Some garden centres have their own expert "plant doctor". Most good tree nurseries should be able to tell you what is wrong with your rhododendrons and what to do about it.

NB: Always take along a few leaves from the diseased shrub when consulting an expert and give him or her exact details of the position and present care of the plant. The same applies when writing for advice.

It is possible to obtain useful insects and alternative pest control agents via the specialist gardening trade and garden mail order firms (enquire at your garden centre).

Propagating rhododendrons

In the wild, rhododendrons and azaleas propagate from seed or from branches which hang down to touch the soil and form roots. Plants can be propagated in the same way in your garden. Try it sometime. It is not as difficult as you may think.

Propagating using hanging branches (layering)

This method is a little time-consuming but nearly always successful. The offspring produced by this method will always have flowers that are exactly like those of the parent plant.

Method

(illustration, see p. 54)
1. In the spring, choose a one- to two-year-old branch, preferably one from the lower part of the shrub and pluck off all the leaves, except for those at the tip. Now lay this branch in a 10-cm (4 in) deep trench or pull it down and cover it so that only the leafy shoot tip sticks up out of the soil.
2. Anchor the shoot in the soil with a U-shaped piece of wire so that it cannot spring back and then fill up the trench with a mixture of leaf mould and peat.
3. After that, all you need is patience. Up to two years may pass before the part of the branch in the ground forms roots.
4. Finally, separate the rooted shoot from the parent plant with sharp clippers, preferably in spring or autumn. The independent young shrub should be carefully dug up and replanted in the chosen position.

My tip: Pinch out the first new shoot of this young plant in the spring so that the shrub will produce more branches.

Propagating from seed

By contrast with the previous method, rhododendron hybrids grown from seed are not necessarily exactly like the parent plant and the offspring may vary to a greater or lesser degree with respect to growth and colour. Usually, only seed from wild species is used for propagating. This method may be of interest to gardeners and rhododendron enthusiasts who wish to experiment with new varieties.

Obtaining seed: Allow a few seedheads to ripen on the chosen shrub. Remove the seedheads in mid- to late autumn and dry them in a flat, open dish at room temperature. Later, store the seed in a closed tin in a cool room.

Sowing time: This will depend on your options.
● In a small greenhouse with some form of heating and light, you may be able to sow seed in late autumn.
● In a propagator without artificial light, you may be able to sow from early spring onwards.
● Outside – if protected by a plastic tunnel – sowing may be successful from the end of spring onwards.

Germination time and temperature: The optimal temperature for germination is somewhere between 10 and 18° C (50-64° F). If you sow the seeds immediately after they have ripened in the autumn, they will germinate within 10-35 days. If sown in spring, it may take up to twelve weeks before the seeds germinate.

Seeding compost and containers: A mixture of peat, rhododendron compost and sand (1:1:1) is very suitable.
Moisten the soil well after mixing. Suitable containers: a propagator or a plastic pot that can be covered with a plate of glass or transparent foil.

A profusion of flowers
Williamsianum hybrid "Oldenburg" with an underplanting of Japanese azaleas and a carpet of saxifrage.

Propagating by layering hanging branches

Defoliate a branch except for the tip, lay it in a 10-cm (4 in) deep trench and anchor it down. Fill the trench with soil so that only the shoot tip is sticking out. After two years the rooted branch can be transplanted.

How to sow
Cover the floor of the seed tray with a 2-cm (¾ in) layer of sand then add the compost on top. Mix it slightly and smooth it over.
1. Distribute the seeds evenly on the surface of the soil, making sure they are not too close together as seedlings growing too densely will develop long necks and become susceptible to fungal disease.
2. Gently press the seeds into the soil but do not cover them over. Moisten them very gently with a fine spray setting.
3. Cover the seed tray with a polythene hood, polythene sheet or a plate of glass. Do not remove the cover until germination has taken place.

Care of the seedlings
During the first few weeks after germination, the seedlings will need a lot of attention to make sure that they do not fall prey to fungal disease.
● Only water them in the mornings and only when the surface of the soil is slightly dry.
● Make sure they are well aired.
● Spray the seedlings with a fungicide every two to four weeks to prevent infestation with fungal disease.
● Provide shade for the seedlings around midday when the sun

becomes stronger in spring.

Thinning out the seedlings: As soon as the first real leaves have developed, following the original two seedling leaves, it will be time to thin out the seedlings and prick them out. If the seed was sown in late autumn, this should be after about two months but it may take up to seven months for seed sown in spring.

Pricking out seedlings
1. Fill a flat wooden tray (tomato box) or large peat pots with seeding compost.
2. Using a dibber, lift a seedling out of the seed tray.
3. Make a hole in the soil with your dibber and place the seedling in it, taking care not to bend or break the little roots.

Propagating from cuttings

4. The pricked-out seedlings should be watered well and placed in a sheltered spot out of doors until the plants have grown to a height of about 10 cm (4 in), after which they can be planted out in a bed.

Propagating from cuttings
Propagating rhododendrons from cuttings is not so easy. Even specialists have difficulties with this method. It seems to work best for Japanese azaleas and a few rhododendron hybrids like "Cunningham's White" and "Catawbiense Grandiflorum".
NB: As a rule, branches that are taken from the centre or lower part of the shrub during late summer/early autumn, will root best.
Method
(see illustration below)
1. Fill flowerpots with a mixture of two parts of peat and one part sand.
2. Cut off several 10-cm (4 in) long branches, preferably without buds, and remove all leaves except for the top four or five.

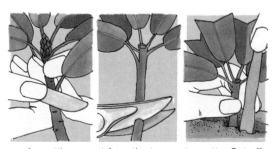

Remove all the leaves of a cutting, apart from the topmost rosette. Cut off the very tip of the shoot and cut off the stem of the cutting below a leaf axil. Push the cutting into a sand-peat compost.

3. Remove the tip of the shoot and use a sharp knife or a pair of scissors to snip off the stem immediately below a leaf axil.

4. Make a slit about 1 cm (⅜ in) long in the bark of the lower end of the stem and dip the slit end in rooting powder (available at garden centres etc.).

5. Make a hole in the soil with your dibber and place the cutting in it up to the leaf axil.

6. Water well and stand the pots in a propagator with underfloor heating. Cover the pots or place inverted jam jars over them and place them on a sunlit windowsill. At constant temperatures of around 21° C (70° F) and in very humid air, the cuttings will take root within a few weeks and certainly by the spring. After that, the cuttings should be placed in a sheltered spot out of doors and gradually toughened up. In spring they can be planted outside.

Propagating by grafting
In grafting, a shoot from one particular rhododendron variety is grafted on to the root of another, more robust species or variety. They will "fuse" together to produce a new plant, which will combine the desired characteristics of both initial plants. In former times, usually only those rhododendron cultivars that were reluctant to develop roots as cuttings were grafted in tree nurseries. Nowadays, most good tree nurseries propagate by grafting all the time, as grafted shrubs usually turn out to be very robust.

Method
(see illustration, above)

1. The base (the shrub with the root) on to which another variety is grafted, is most often supplied by the large-flowered hybrid "Cunningham's White". This variety has a particularly strong and

Grafting

Choose a robust base plant and cut it off a hand's width above the neck of the roots. Make a diagonal cut on both the base plant and the grafting plant, so that they will fit neatly together. Place both parts together and bind them tightly with cotton tape or rubberized grafting tape.

healthy root system. The best speciman to choose is the root of a one-year-old plant, grown from a cutting, which has the previous year's shoot from the rhododendron variety of your choice as the part grafted on to the base.

2. The best time for grafting is early spring.

3. Six weeks before grafting, you should plant the base plant in a pot filled with special rhododendron compost and stand it in a flowerbed.

4. Immediately before grafting, cut off the top of the plant you are going to use as a base, just about a hand's width above the neck of the roots, and then, using a sharp knife, make a diagonal cut in the stem.

5. Now choose a shoot from the plant you are going to graft on to the base, making sure the thickness of its stem corresponds as closely as possible to that of the base plant. Now cut this stem diagonally at the same angle as you cut the first stem.

6. Place the two diagonally cut surfaces together so that they fit neatly. In time, a callus will form in the cambium layer beneath the bark, caused by a secretion produced by the wounds, which will help the base and the grafted plant to fuse

together, making a strong join.

7. Firmly bind up the grafted join with cotton tape or rubberized grafting tape which can be bought in the gardening trade.

Care after grafting: Place the newly grafted plant in a cold frame or greenhouse. As long as it takes for the grafted section to fuse with the base, the plant will require temperatures of 18-22° C (64-71° F) and very high humidity. During this period – about six weeks – keep the cold frame lid shut. Provide shade in sunny weather.

After this time, air the plant more frequently and fertilize once or twice before the beginning of summer. In the middle of the first month of summer, the young plant can be planted out in a sheltered position in the garden.

NB: Further details about grafting or propagating from cuttings and seed can be found in specialist literature devoted to this subject. Ask at your local library, book shop or garden centre.

Mixed planting

A rhododendron bed can be rounded off elegantly by planting suitable neigbours. Bushes, flowering herbaceous plants, ornamental ferns, grasses and bulbs will make sure that the bed is attractive from spring right through to the autumn. It is important that the colours of the flowering plants should all blend together well and that they have the same requirements with respect to position and soil.

When you begin to plan your rhododendron plantation, you should think a little about accompanying plants. Neighbouring plants give a bed variety, provide a frame, add colour before and after the flowering time of the rhododendrons and make care easier. Depending on their height and character, they will fulfil several different aims.

Trees: form the basic framework of a plantation, into which all other plants are fitted. You will find suggestions for small trees and flowering trees and shrubs in the tables on pages 58/59. Taller trees, which will provide shade, are listed on page 15.

Conifers and evergreen trees and bushes will blend in well with rhododendrons, partly because they have similar requirements in respect to position. The pillar-like or pyramid-shaped growth of many conifers gives an optical contrast and provides variety when grown together with the rather rounded to spreading rhododendron shrubs.

Flowering bushes – many flower at the same time as rhododendrons, while others also bring added interest into the plantation with their varied flower shapes and colours. Early- or later-flowering varieties are the most important providers of colour.

Herbaceous plants will set off the splendid flowers of rhododendrons and will definitely guarantee that the plantation does not lack attractive features later on in the year. Ornamental-leaved herbaceous plants, which also have attractive flowers, will provide interest all summer with their decorative foliage.

Bulbs play an important role in the spring when nothing else is flowering and make good neighbours for early-flowering rhododendron varieties.

Shade-providing grasses and ferns, being forest dwellers, are naturally suitable as neighbours for rhododendrons. Their elegant growth and delicate foliage create an attractive effect among the underplanting.

Ground-cover plants are prostrate herbaceous plants and woody plants which generally propagate by means of stolons and soon create a beautiful thick carpet. They keep the ground moist and loose and prevent the proliferation of weeds. From the point of view of design, they are the basis for the plantation, which links all the other plants one with another.

Designing a mixed bed

Think of a painting when you are planning the shape of your plantation. First, there is the frame, provided by trees and taller conifers. Among these are placed shrubs, including rhododendrons and low-growing conifers. Now add the herbaceous plants, grasses and ferns. Right at the end, fill the empty spaces with ground-covering plants. If you wish to have spring bulbs as well, you will have to plant them later on, in the autumn.

Choosing plants

To avoid creating a motley collection or a kind of botanical garden rather than one harmonious picture, you should use several specimens of some of the plants.

General rule: The larger the plant, the less individuals will be needed. In the case of trees, large conifers and tall bushes, one example will be sufficient. Smaller shrubs and herbaceous plants should be planted in groups of two or three or more, depending on how much space you have. No fewer than seven to nine specimens of ground-covering plants should be used together if the end result is not to look like a patchwork quilt.

Elegant ferns and a variety of hostas make particularly decorative companion plants for the rhododendron bed.

Choosing colours

It is your choice of colours that will utimately determine whether your plant composition looks harmonious or not. Blue and white flowers look good with all the typical rhododendron shades and you can hardly go wrong if you choose accompanying plants that flower in these colours. Be more cautious with pink. Most shades of pink go very well with many of the large-flowered rhododendrons and Japanese azaleas but do not look quite as tasteful with the glowing shades of orange and yellow displayed by the deciduous varieties of azaleas. Deep or bright pink rhdodendrons do not go well with yellow neighbours. Of course, this only applies if the accompanying plants flower at the same time as the rhododendrons.

A profusion of shapes

Combining contrasting shapes can add interest to your plantation: delicate fern fronds beside the large-leaved foliage of hosta; graceful grass stalks placed in front of the dense, compact foliage mounds of *Rhododendron yakushimanum*. Such contrasts can provide your plantation with plenty to catch the eye even if nothing happens to be flowering at the moment.

Companion plants

Acer palmatum

Pieris japonica

Hydrangea macrophylla

Here you will find a selection of suitable neighbouring plants. Details are given on how tall each particular plant may grow and what shape it will have. The flowering time and colours of flowering shrubs and plants are also indicated.

✝ This plant is toxic!

Ornamental trees

Japanese maple
(Acer palmatum)
4 m (160 in) tall, funnel-shaped growth; the foliage has beautiful autumn colouring.

Cornus florida
4-6 m (160-240 in) tall; flowers late spring/early summer; white flowers, or pink flowers in the variety "Rubra".

Japanese witch hazel
(Hamamelis japonica)
2.5-3.5 m (98-138 in) tall, funnel-shaped upright, very slow growth; yellow flowers from mid- winter to mid-spring.

Laburnum ✝
(Laburnum "Vossii")
5-7 m (200-280 in) tall, golden yellow flowers on racemes in late spring/ early summer. Very attractive with deciduous azaleas.
Warning: All parts of the plant are extremely toxic!

Magnolia
(Magnolia kobus)
8-10 m (320-400 in) tall, 10-cm (4 in) flowers in mid- to late spring, conspicuous red fruits.

Ornamental cherry
(Prunus sargentii and serrulata varieties)
Depending on the species or variety, 3-7 m (120-280 in) tall; foliage with beautiful autumn clours. Luxuriant pink or white flowers in mid-spring, late spring or early summer.

Conifers and evergreen trees

False cypress
(Chamaecyparis spp.)
Conifer with a rounded, pyramid or pillar shape; depending on the species or variety 0.5-10 m (20-400 in) tall, with yellow, green or bluish needles.

Mountain laurel ✝
(Kalmia latifolia)
Bushy shrub, 1.5-2 m (60-80 in) tall; pink flower umbels in late spring/early summer.
Warning: The leaves and seeds are toxic!

Leucothoe catesbaei
A 1-m (40 in) tall shrub with creeping shoots and white flower panicles in mid-spring.

Pieris japonica ✝
Spreading, upright bush; 2-3 m (80-120 in) tall with creamy white flower panicles from early to late spring.
Warning: All parts of the plant are toxic!

Skimmia
(Skimmie x foremanii)
50-cm (20 in) tall, semi-spherical bush with laurel-like berries. Pinkish-white flower panicles in mid- to late-spring, decorative red berries in the autumn.

Eastern or Canada hemlock
(Tsuga canadensis "Nana" or "Jeddeloh")
50-cm (20 in) tall dwarf conifer with cushion-like growth and gently drooping branches.

Flowering shrubs

Hydrangea ✝
(Hydrangea macrophylla)
1-2 m (40-80 in) tall; compact shrub with large bluish or pink flower clusters in mid-summer.
Warning: All parts of the plant are toxic!

Hydrangea ✝
(Hydrangea paniculata "Grandiflora")
Upright growth, 2 m (80 in) tall. White, lilac-like flower spikes in late summer.
Warning: All parts of the plant are toxic!

Enkiathus campanulatus
2-3 m (80-120 in) tall, with branches arranged in storeys. Reddish bell-shaped flowers in late spring. Red foliage in autumn.

Magnolia
(Magnolia sieboldii)
1.5-2.5 m (60-100 in) tall. Flowers in mid-summer, white with striking red stamens.

Magnolia
(Magnolia stellata)
Broad, bushy 2-m (80 in) tall shrub with white, fragrant, star-shaped flowers in early to mid-spring; beautiful light green foliage.

Viburnum plicatum "Mariesii" ✝
Up to 2 m (80 in) tall with broad, spreading growth; large, flat, white flower umbels in mid-spring.
Warning: All parts of the plant, especially the berries, are toxic!

Hosta

Endymion non-scriptus

Polystichum setiferum

Cornus canadensis

Herbaceous plants

Astilbe
(Astilbe)
40-80-cm (16 in) tall herbaceous plant with graceful foliage and white, pink and fiery red flower spikes in mid- and late summer.

Bergenia
(Bergenia)
20-40-cm (8-16 in) tall, large, roundish leaves; white, pink and red flower sprays in mid-spring.

Hosta
(Hosta varieties and species)
Decorative blue, green, yellow or white variegated leaves. In summer or autumn blue or white flowers.

Iris sibirica
80-100 cm (32-40 in) tall; elegant, narrow leaves; blue, white or pink flowers in early summer.

Japanese primrose
(Primula japonica)
50 cm (20 in) tall; varieties have red, orange, pink and white flowers; flowering time early to late summer.

Peltiphyllum peltatum
80 cm (32 in) tall, decorative-leaved herbaceous plant with pink flower umbels in late spring.

Rodgersia varieties
Large, round or umbrella-shaped leaves, depending on the variety; creamy white flowers in early to mid-summer.

Bulbs

Fritillary ☫
(Fritillaria meleagris)
20-cm (8 in) high; purple to white, checkered, bell-shaped flowers in mid-spring.
Warning: The bulb is toxic!

Erythronium varieties
Cyclamen-like, nodding flowers in mid-spring, white, pink or yellow.

Summer snowflake ☫
(Leucojum aestivum)
30 cm (12 in) tall, with white lily-of-the-valley-type flowers in late spring.
Warning: The bulbs are toxic!

Lilies
(Lilium speciosum, L. auratum, L. pardalinum)
Varieties that like acid soil, all varieties over 1 m (40 in) tall; flower in mid- to late summer.

Narcissus ☫
(Narcissus species and varieties)
30-50 cm (12-20 in) tall; yellow, white or multi-coloured flowers in mid- to late-spring.
Warning: All parts of the plant, but particularly the bulb, are toxic!

Bluebell ☫
(Endymion non-scriptus)
20-30 cm (8-12 in) tall, with blue, bell-shaped flowers in late spring/early summer. Particularly valuable as it proliferates very quickly.
Warning: The seeds and the bulb are toxic!

Grasses and ferns

Carex morrowii "Variegata"
30 cm (12 in) tall; white-striped, evergreen leaves.

Sedge
(Carex plantaginea)
30 cm (12 in) tall; broad fresh green leaves; evergreen.

Giant fescue
(Festuca gigantea)
100 cm (40 in) tall; fresh green leaves; hanging flowers.

Ostrich fern
(Matteuccia struthiopteris)
80 cm (32 in) tall; light green leaves arranged in a funnel shape. Will form stolons.

Athyrium niponicum "Metallicum"
50 cm (20 in) tall; striking, silvery-red fronds.

Soft shield fern
(Polystichum setiferum "Proliferum")
40 cm (16 in) tall; narrow fronds that are feathered in three sections, winter-green.

Ground-cover plants

Bugle
(Ajuga reptans)
Vigorously growing herbaceous plant with oval leaves that are green, dark purple or pinkish-white, depending on the variety. The flowers are blue or white and appear in late spring.

Cornus canadensis
20 cm (8 in) tall; white, star-shaped flowers on fresh green foliage in late spring.

Creeping wintergreen
(Gaultheria procumbens)
Dwarf shrub that forms stolons; has red berries and small, evergreen leaves.

Blue-eyed Mary
(Omphalodes verna)
Herbaceous plant which forms stolons. Flowers in mid- to late spring; flowers are sky blue or white.

Pyrenean saxifrage
(Saxifraga umbrosa)
Quickly forms thick carpets of dark green leaf rosettes. In late spring, delicate white flower spikes appear.

Waldsteinia ternata
Winter-green herbaceous plant with yellow flowers in mid- to late spring; leaves similar to those of strawberries.

Index

Figures given in bold indicate illustrations.

Index

Index

Index

Glossary

cutting - part of a plant that has been cut off for propagating purposes. In the case of rhododendrons, use the shoot tip.

evergreen - plants that remain green all year round and only lose their oldest leaves in spring or autumn.

humidity - the amount of water in the air:
  0% = completely dry air;
  100% = saturated, misty air.
Rhododendrons feel most comfortable in air containing 70% humidity.

hybrids - plants created by crossing different species or varieties or, more rarely, genera. These new plants combine the positive characteristics of the parent plants. Hybrids are often particularly colourful, large-flowered and healthy.

inflorescence - cluster of flowers; can be described as open or dense, consisting of a certain number of individual flowerheads.

peat - a humus-rich potting soil consisting of semi-decomposed peat mosses and moorland plants, used for improving the structure of ordinary soils and for lowering the pH factor. As moorland/wetland is destroyed when peat is extracted, it should be used sparingly and, if possible, other compost should be substituted, for example, leaf mould or bark compost.

pH factor - on a scale of 0-14, this gives a degree of chemical reaction in the acid-neutral-alkaline ranges. Values below 7 indicate acid soil; values above 7 indicate alkaline soil. A value of 7 is neutral.

seedling - a young plant grown from seed.

soil - matter in which plants grow, for example, garden soil, bark compost or peat. In practical terms, this word is often used to describe specially prepared and mixed soil rather than ordinary garden soil.

taxonomy - botanists have developed a system for classifying plants which includes all growing plants. It is divided up into families, then genera and species. If new plants are created by crossing different varieties of the same species, these are called cultivars or varieties.

trace elements - nutrients which are only required by plants in very small quantities, but without which healthy growth is impossible. Among the most important trace elements are iron, magnesiuim, boron, copper and molybdenum. These elements occur naturally in soil but must be replaced on a regular basis in long-term plantations.

veins - the more or less clearly visible web of veins through which a leaf is supplied with water and nutrients.

waterlogging - this occurs when surplus water in the soil cannot drain away properly. This creates a deficiency of oxygen in the soil and the plants' roots begin to decay.

Cover photographs
Front cover: *Hybrid "Purple Splendour".*
Inside front cover: *Large-flowered hybrids.*
Inside back cover: *Deciduous azaleas "Tunis", "Madame" and "Jolie".*
Back cover: *Japanese azalea "Favorite".*

Photographic acknowledgements
Blatterspiel: Page 31, top left, top centre; CD-Photo: Page 58 centre; The Garden Picture Library: front cover; Hachmann: page 2, 8, 12, 17, 22, 24, 25, 26 top, 26 bottom right, 27 top, 28, 29 top, 29 bottom left, 31 bottom left, 32, 33, 34 left, 34 centre, 35 left, centre left, centre right, 48; Kögel: page 16, 43, 53, 59 left; Lehmann: page 3 bottom, 58 left; Mein schöner Garten/Fischer: page 5, 47, back cover; mein schöner Garten/Kögel: page 3 top, 59 centre left; Mein schöner Garten/Krieg: page 39; Nickig: page 19; Riedmiller: page 59 right, Schlaback: page 11; Stork: page 56, 59 centre right; Stöckmann: page 26 bottom left, 27 bottom, 29 bottom right, 34 right; Strauss: page 4, 20, 21 top left, top centre, top right, bottom left, bottom centre, bottom right, 30, 31 top right, 31 bottom centre, 31 bottom right, 35 right, inside back cover.

This edition published 1994 by
Merehurst Limited
Ferry House, 51-57 Lacy Road,
Putney, London SW15 1PR
Reprinted 1995, 1996

© 1989 Gräfe und Unzer GmbH, Munich

ISBN 1 85391 317 0

A catalogue record for this book is available from the British Library.

English text copyright ©
Merehurst Limited 1994
Translated by Astrid Mick
Edited by Lesley Young
Design and typesetting by
Paul Cooper Design
Illustrations by Ushie Dorner
Printed in Hong Kong by
Wing King Tong Ltd